PURPOSE DRIVEN LEGACY

Living a life worthy of legacy

PURPOSE DRIVEN LEGACY

Living a life worthy of legacy

DUSTIN ROYER

PALMETTO
PUBLISHING
Charleston, SC
www.PalmettoPublishing.com

© 2024 by Dustin Royer

All rights reserved

No portion of this book may be reproduced, stored in a retrieval system, or transmitted in any form by any means— electronic, mechanical, photocopy, recording, or other— except for brief quotations in printed reviews, without prior permission of the author.

Paperback ISBN: 979-8-8229-4823-5
eBook ISBN: 979-8-8229-4824-2

CONTENTS

FOREWORD 1	*vii*
FOREWORD 2	*x*
PREFACE	*xii*
INTRODUCTION	*1*
MY JOURNEY	*5*
GODLY LEGACY	*26*
PRIORITIES	*31*
PRIORITY 1: YOUR WALK WITH JESUS	*35*
PRIORITY 2: YOUR SPOUSE	*54*
PRIORITY 3: YOUR FAMILY	*77*
PRIORITY 4: YOUR WORK	*84*
PRIORITY 5: YOUR MINISTRY	*92*
APPLICATION	*99*
CONCLUSION	*104*
ACKNOWLEDGMENT AND THANK YOU	*106*
APPENDIX	*108*
SCRIPTURE INDEX	*111*

FOREWORD 1

The late poet L. W. Rice once penned the words, "A man has left a path of words beside the road he trod." Therefore, it could be said that everything we learned, all we know, and the wholeness of what we shall leave someday were and are best displayed by the words that burst upon our mind the moment we think of the past that influenced us, the present that directs our daily endeavors, and the future memories we desire to surround the minds of generations to come when they think of us.

In this masterful work, Dustin Royer raises, from the depths of our lives, a list of words that no legacy left to the reader or desired legacy we hope to bequeath upon our future could ignore, preserve, or pass on without allowing each word to marinate our conscious thought.

As the author is my own nephew, I had a front-row seat to much of his childhood, teen years, military career, and adult family creation and journey. Although not savvy to all the details the author shares but aware of many, I was newly enlightened, engaged, and often awed at how each important part of his life affected his feelings at the time. Better yet, I know how he unreservedly reveals and declares his personal transformation from the hands of a wonderful, loving, all-seeing, and caring God, Lord, and Savior, Jesus Christ.

Upon reading the first few pages of the original manuscript, I quickly grabbed my pen and began to write the words that jumped off the pages. I knew I was receiving a personal message and needed guidance from not only a gifted, competent writer but also from the same source of inspiration that had traveled from his eyes and ears to his mind and eventually his hand.

The words in the list could each be a subject of another book or study, but I soon realized no legacy given, received, or passed on could measure its value without taking the key words the author lays before us and asking three personal questions. First, how did I see that word displayed (good, bad, or not at all) in my impressionable life growing up? Second, how do my family and friends see me display the best use of each of these words? Third, at my memorial service or long after I have left this life, will my name declare that I used each of these principles in a way that my legacy had purpose and that purpose will have saved others from pain?

The words that are the stepping stones for self-examination and desired destination are: priority, identity, healing, restoration, spouse, family, generational, work, trust, ministry, effectiveness, action, sonship, principles, mercy, talent, abilities, relationship, time, companionship, alignment, compassion, humility, awareness, forgiveness, example, prayer, devotion accountability, pursuit, and my favorite, BLUF, which I learned was a military acronym for Bottom Line Up Front.

The words are dealt with so beautifully and clearly that if you will do the reflection and application work at the end of each chapter, it will take you on a journey of your own to see how these vital aspects of your life were displayed in the legacy handed to you? Good or bad, what is the next generation learning from you? And most importantly, what kind of legacy will you leave everyone, from your closest family to the most casual observer?

So I would say to my author nephew, "In my over three-quarters of a century of life, your Uncle Sam may have never read a more needed, inspiring, and life-changing book than *Purpose-Driven Legacy*." I challenge you: read on, do not stop, do the work, and answer your own questions. And if you do, I have every reason to believe you may say the same about this book.

—Samuel P. Pawlak Sr. (Uncle Sam)

FOREWORD 2

Dear Dustin,

I was truly honored and deeply moved to receive your book. The trust you've placed in me by asking me to write the foreword is both humbling and inspiring. I want you to know that your work has profoundly touched my heart and resonated with my own aspirations and reflections on legacy. I want to apologize that I did not get to read it until yesterday and just finished it today.

As I turned each page, I found myself drawn into the depth of your insights and the practical wisdom you've shared on creating a lasting legacy. It's rare to come across a work that not only enlightens but also compels one to take immediate action. Your book has done just that for me. I am genuinely moved to implement several of your practices in my own life, underscoring my desire to leave a meaningful legacy for my children and our grandchildren and those I have the privilege to influence.

Please accept my heartfelt gratitude for the impact your book has already made in my life. I am looking forward to penning the foreword, not only as a contribution to your powerful work but as a personal testament to the significance it holds for me. Your book is a gift for all of us aspiring to leave behind something of true value. It made me love you more and know you at a deeper level.

Thank you for who you are and helping birth SeaGlass Church. Without your family, I don't know where our church would be. I am looking forward to sitting with you soon. I also look forward to sharing how much your book has influenced me with others.

Honored that we are family,

David Oates, senior pastor, SeaGlass Church

PREFACE

A LETTER TO MY DAD

As I stand at the threshold of presenting this book to the world, I find myself grappling with a delicate balance between honesty and reverence, particularly when it comes to discussing the role of my father in shaping the narrative of purposeful living and leaving a Godly legacy.

In these pages, I share deeply personal reflections and anecdotes from my life, woven intricately with lessons learned, challenges faced, and victories celebrated. At times, these reflections may cast shadows upon the image of my father, and for this, I feel compelled to offer a preface of understanding and empathy.

I want the readers to know that my earthly father is a good father. There are times in our lives where we don't put enough emphasis on the good things. I always knew my dad loved me, and I love him very much too.

While it is true that some of the details recounted here may portray my father in a light that appears harsh or critical, it is essential to recognize the complexity of human relationships and the multifaceted nature of familial dynamics. My intention in sharing these moments is not to disparage or diminish the love and support that my father provided throughout my life, but rather to illuminate the journey of growth and transformation that we embarked upon together.

My father was, and continues to be, a pillar of strength and wisdom in my life. His guidance, love, and unwavering belief in the power of faith have shaped me in profound ways, laying the foundation for the principles of purpose and legacy that are at the heart of this book. It is with deep respect and gratitude that I honor his legacy within these pages, recognizing that our shared experiences, both joyful and challenging, have ultimately contributed to the person I am today.

In offering this preface, I invite readers to approach the stories contained herein with an open heart and a spirit of understanding. May the lessons gleaned from my journey serve as a testament to the enduring power of love, forgiveness, and the pursuit of purposeful living in leaving a lasting legacy grounded in faith.

With humility and reverence, your son,
Dustin

INTRODUCTION

What would Jesus say about you if he were invited to speak at your memorial service? Would he recognize you as one of his own? Would he speak of the moments when your heart resonated with his teachings, or would he share the times he saw himself in your acts of love and compassion?

That is the question I have asked myself a lot lately. What kind of legacy am I leaving behind? Am I being purposeful in building a Godly legacy that will have a long-lasting impact on my family and friends?

Would Jesus say that he knows me?

I have felt the Lord encouraging me to write about legacy from my perspective for quite some time. I want to say a few things right out of the gate before I get started. This book is deeply personal, and I will share stories and memories I have never shared with anyone else. I want it to be real. I want it to be relevant. I want it to be inspired by God, and I want it to make a difference in your life. There are churches, pastors, ministries, and people that I speak about throughout this book that are important to the story and to the message. However, to protect their integrity, I will not mention any of those elements by name unless I have explicitly received permission from them.

If, at any point in writing this, I start to feel that there is too much of me writing and that God is not inspiring it, I commit to stop, listen, fast, and seek inspiration and guidance on how and whether I should proceed.

I pray that this book brings you as much joy in reading it as it did me in writing it.

Unless otherwise noted, all scripture references throughout this book are taken from the Christian Standard Bible (CSB). If you are unfamiliar with the CSB, it is a very accurate translation designed to be read at a seventh-grade reading level. I feel refreshed reading this version of the Bible and have found that the simplicity of the wording is much easier to understand and apply in my life.

The website csbible.com says this of the CSB: "The result is a Bible that shines by academic standards and is remarkably enjoyable to read—The Christian Standard Bible. The CSB employs a translation philosophy called Optimal Equivalence, which seeks to achieve an optimal balance of linguistic precision with contemporary clarity." [1] [2]

WHAT IS LEGACY?

The dictionary definition of "legacy" is an amount of money or property left to someone in a will. It is the long-lasting impact of particular events, actions, etcetera, that occurred in the past in a person's life.[3]

Most simply stated, every person wants to be remembered, and legacy is what they leaves behind. Everyone will leave behind a legacy of some kind. That fact is inevitable, but what will be said of you? Who will remember you? What will they remember? What have you left behind?

Our family has a group chat that we use to communicate. We call it "Da Fam Chat," and it comprises all our immediate family members:

---

1 "Holman Handcrafted Bible Collection." CSB, October 18, 2023. https://csbible.com/holman-handcrafted-bible-collection/.

2 "FAQ." CSB, July 24, 2019. https://csbible.com/about-the-csb/faqs/#faq/may-i-use-the-christian-standard-bible-in-my-writing.

3 "Legacy Definition & Usage Examples." Dictionary.com. Accessed April 1, 2024. https://www.dictionary.com/browse/legacy.

my wife, Sandra, and me; my oldest daughter, Dana, and her husband; my youngest daughter, Leah, and her husband; and my son, Elijah. We all send each other text updates, pictures of the grandbabies and dogs, etcetera. Sandra and I like to send encouragement and scriptures as the Lord puts them in our hearts.

One day, I came across this scripture in Hebrews while writing an encouragement text for our family group chat: "No discipline seems enjoyable at the time, but painful. Later on, however, it yields the fruit of peace and righteousness to those who have been trained by it" (Heb. 12:11).

It is easy to look at this passage, see the word *discipline*, and immediately think of correction. You may even be reminded of a time when your father or mother fussed at you about something you did. You may think I sent that scripture to my family group chat to discipline them for something they did or didn't do that needed correction. You likely received punishment of some sort and associate the word discipline with that punishment. As painful as they may be, these moments are essential because we often learn more from our mistakes than our successes.

However, there is another relevant meaning when we choose to be purposeful in what we leave behind.

Proverbs 23:12 describes a type of discipline: "Apply yourself to discipline and listen to words of knowledge."

The Greek word for discipline is Egkrateia, which means "self-control, power over oneself." [4]

The Latin word for discipline is *disciplina*, meaning "to teach, guide, and instruct." [5]

---

[4] "G1466 - Egkrateia - Strong's Greek Lexicon (KJV)." Blue Letter Bible. Accessed April 1, 2024. https://www.blueletterbible.org/lexicon/g1466/kjv/tr/0-1/.

[5] Mahoney, Kevin D. "Latin Search Results for: Disciplina." Latin Definitions for: disciplina (Latin Search) - Latin Dictionary and Grammar Resources - Latdict. Accessed April 1, 2024. https://www.latin-dictionary.net/search/latin/disciplina.

Now I admit, I am not a Greek or Latin scholar, but I find that knowing the root meaning of the word *discipline* is essential to fully understanding this passage and what it means to the process of building a purposeful legacy.

- A purposeful legacy requires *enkrateia*. You must have self-control and be purposeful in building an impactful legacy.
- You must *disciplina* your family and friends to carry on and build their purposeful legacy.

I was forty-seven when I started hearing the Lord ask me to write about legacy. At that point, I was well on the path of life and building a legacy, but I had never been intentional about the result. This book will contain many personal testimonies and stories about my journey that I hope you can relate to and that inspire you in building your legacy. I am not a perfect vessel by any means; I am far from it.

> *I have been crucified with Christ; it is no longer I who live, but Christ lives in me; and the life which I now live in the flesh, I live by faith in the Son of God, who loved me and delivered himself up for me.*
> —Galatians 2:20

To the Jesus inside me…take the wheel.

MY JOURNEY

Is there power in our testimony? Let's see what the Word says about it:

> What was from the beginning, what we have heard, what we have seen with our eyes, what we have observed and have touched with our hands, concerning the word of life—that life was revealed, and we have seen it and we testify and declare to you the eternal life that was with the Father and was revealed to us—what we have seen and heard we also declare to you, so that you may also have fellowship with us; and indeed our fellowship is with the Father and with his Son, Jesus Christ. We are writing these things so that our joy may be complete. —(1 John 1:1–4)

So I ask again: Is there power in our testimony? Consider this: If the disciples had not shared their personal experiences with us, would we be here today?

Yes, there is power in sharing our testimony!

I must share my testimony and journey to convey my perspective. It's the most authentic way I know to bridge the gap and articulate the unique viewpoint that has been placed upon my heart. Sharing my journey is immensely personal and vulnerable. Still, it is a path I believe the Lord has set me upon, urging me to explore the concept of legacy through the experience of my own lenses so that you may benefit from it and build a Godly legacy.

I grew up in a loving Christian household deeply rooted in ministry. Many of my family members were actively involved in various aspects of it. One notable figure among them was my great-uncle, Rex Humbard, a renowned televangelist whose ministry, at its prime, I have been told, reached more people globally than even Billy Graham. His legacy was genuinely remarkable. Also, on my mother's side, my grandfather, affectionately known as "Poppy," was a full-time ordained minister with the Assemblies of God. My uncle Allen served as an Episcopal priest and counselor, and my mother, gifted with a remarkably anointed voice, recorded several gospel albums during her youth under the Humbard label.

On my father's side, my father, my aunt Pat, my uncle Sam, my cousins Sammy and April and her husband, and my Uncle Mike are all, or were all, ordained ministers with the Assemblies of God. My Uncle Mike was a minister and rabbi with extensive knowledge of Hebrew and Greek origins, and my Uncle Sam is one of the most well-read, intelligent, and Godly men I have ever known. Even those family members who didn't pursue full-time ministry were actively involved in worship and various ministries throughout their lives. I share these family connections to emphasize that I hail from a lineage of devoted Christ followers, all of whom have positively influenced my life and the lives of so many.

I want to begin with a vivid childhood memory that's etched in my mind. My grandfather, "Poppy," served as the pastor of a church in Venice, Florida, for many years. When I was a young child, that church building felt immense. At the back of the stage, were these large green curtains with an opening in the center, concealing a hallway with rooms at each end. These rooms served as classrooms for the children's church and Royal Rangers.

Behind those curtains, on both sides, were a couple of green-and-yellow couches. During the church service, I often found myself on those couches, clutching drumsticks in my hands, a drum throne in front of me. With unwavering enthusiasm, I would enthusiastically accompany the worship team; listening to the music, I would try my best to replicate every drumbeat. My father would be playing the piano, harmonizing beautifully with my mother; both were gifted with incredible voices. Meanwhile, my grandmother would gracefully play the organ or the vibraharp, and Poppy, with his guitar, would join in. Occasionally, my Uncle Danny, my greatest hero, would visit and take his place behind the drums. His drumming skills were awe-inspiring, and I aspired to be like him.

At a certain point early in my childhood, we relocated about an hour north to Tampa because my dad had taken a job managing a Radio Shack near MacDill Air Force Base. My mom worked in the same shopping center and managed the Sears Surplus store a few storefronts away. From my young perspective, those years held a special charm. Radio Shack was a treasure trove of the most excellent RC cars, computers, and video games, while Sears stocked all the GI Joes and Transformers a kid could dream of. We didn't attend church regularly, and I recall visiting various churches intermittently.

Amid the backdrop of my toy-filled world, my parents' relationship was strained, marked by frequent arguments. As a young child, I remained blissfully unaware of the unfolding turmoil around me. Then, one fateful day, everything unraveled. It's a memory etched in my mind as vividly as if it happened yesterday. My sister and I eagerly assisted my mom in making homemade doughnuts, planning to surprise our dad at his workplace. His return from one of his monthly business trips to Orlando thrilled us. We packed up everything and headed to the store to deliver our surprise.

I can still see my mother's face to this day when she walked in and discovered that he was with the woman with whom he had been having an affair. I remember the tears in her eyes as she said, "Let's go." I cried because I wanted to see my daddy, not understanding that he had been having an affair with another woman for some time. Later, I learned that all those supposed work trips were excuses to spend weekends with his mistress. And just like that, my parents were suddenly divorced, and my world was turned upside down.

Shortly after the divorce, my father married her, and we moved back to Venice, Florida, with my mom. My mom eventually remarried, and we relocated to Sarasota, Florida, with my new stepdad. With time, the wounds from the past began to heal, and God's grace shone through. I always felt the love of both parents, and as the years passed, I grew to love and respect my stepmom and stepdad. I also started to notice how well my parents got along with each other, a bond that remains strong to this day.

My dad regularly visited; we saw him every Thursday and spent every other weekend with him. During this time, he became involved in a church in Brandon, Florida, taking on a role in worship leadership. He placed a keyboard on stage next to him, though it wasn't connected to anything except a small amp for me to learn to play alongside him and the band. When we were home with my mom, I'd return from school and spend hours playing the drums with my boombox to its maximum volume. Interestingly, the drums were the same set that had once been at my Poppy's church when I was a kid. He gave them to me, and I poured my heart into playing them over the years.

My sister and I spent the summer with my dad between my ninth- and tenth-grade years of high school. He and I spent most of the summer jamming in a small bedroom he used as a music room. He played the keys while I played along on the drums. One memorable Wednesday night, the church's regular drummer couldn't attend the service. My dad said, "Dusty, sit down at the drumkit and give me a beat." I must have done a decent job that night because from then on, I found myself behind the drum set, and over time, I became quite proficient at it.

That summer, as all boys do, I had a few crushes on a couple of girls I met in the youth group and discovered the most beautiful and fun girl I had ever met. It's funny how God's plan unfolds; I can't help but laugh as I type this. I had been talking to one girl, and I remember going to her house to watch a movie. That night, though, I sensed she wasn't interested in pursuing a relationship with me. While hanging out at her home, I found that her sister and I got along remarkably well. That night, she gave me the classic "Hey, I can't be in a relationship right now because I need to focus on Jesus" line.

As the summer ended, and as I entered my sophomore year of high school, I was torn between staying with my dad, where I had made some great friends at church, and returning to my mom's house, where I had no friends. It was a tough decision, and I worried about hurting my mom in the process, but she loved me so much that she wanted nothing more than for me to be happy. Shortly after moving back to my dad's house, I started talking to the most beautiful girl in the world, who happened to be the little sister of the girl I had tried to date earlier, and she became the love of my life.

The air force years: I joined the US Air Force in Sep 1995, and after basic training and tech school, I was stationed at Barksdale AFB in Louisianna. In June of 1997, I married the love of my life, Sandra. She graduated from high school one weekend, and the following weekend, we were married, packed up our stuff, and were off to Shreveport. Joining the air force was one of my better decisions, as it gave me the discipline, order, and stability required to provide for my family. The skills and education I acquired in those years set us on a path to financial stability, allowing my wife to stay home and raise three wonderful, God-loving children. As of the date I wrote this, we have been married for over twenty-six years and have three children, two granddaughters, and another one on the way. Even though those were some very challenging years, we made it through. God has been so good to our family.

After my military service, we returned home and bought our first house in Riverview, Florida. We attempted to reconnect with our childhood church, only to discover it no longer resonated with us. We felt the need to seek guidance from the Lord, and during this season, he led us to a remarkable, spirit-filled church where we formed strong bonds of friendship with families we knew from the old church. I became actively involved in the worship team, while Sandra took on a role in the nursery while pregnant with our second child, Leah.

One Friday evening, we visited a new church that my dad and stepmom had recently begun attending, and we immediately felt a calling to be a part of this start-up process. I met with our pastor and shared that we felt called to join the new church but requested that he be the one to dedicate our daughter, Leah, who was just a few months old at the time. His response left a profound impact on me. He said, "Dustin, I would be honored to dedicate your little one. I want you to know that it has been a real pleasure shepherding your family during this season, and you are only mine to shepherd until the Lord calls you into something greater." There was no pressure to stay or bolster his congregation, which was remarkable.

The new church was vibrant and full of passionate individuals devoted to serving God. The congregation had outgrown its building; every service was packed with people eager to worship. The worship experience was incredible, the messages were inspiring, and it felt like a spiritual home. During this time, we formed deep and lasting friendships with people whom we remain in close contact with today. These friends are the very individuals I want to share my legacy with.

The little church's vibrancy became so well-known locally that a large megachurch in Brandon, Florida, just twenty minutes up the road, which had recently lost its pastor, expressed interest in having our pastor become their new leader. His response was remarkable: he would not leave us behind. Instead, we embarked on a journey to merge two churches into a new season with a new identity.

While some challenges were involved in merging two churches, I felt it the most where I actively served, in the integration of two worship teams. Both teams were exceptional teams, comprised of talented musicians and singers. But when they were meshed together, it was tough to establish order. In the first few weeks, our stage resembled a modern large symphony orchestra, with multiple guitarists, drummers, keyboardists, percussionists, and singers. Over time, we established rotations and settled into a fantastic worship team.

I learned a lot in those years and became an exceptional drummer and bass player. I knew how good I had gotten, and it became my identity. When introducing myself to someone new, I would say, "I'm Dustin; I'm *the* drummer." Although I didn't emphasize the word the to them, in my head, I was saying that I was *the* drummer. I wanted to be the best and was willing to put in the time to do it. To say I was arrogant is an understatement, whether it showed in my outward expressions or not. People started to notice how good I had gotten and would often compliment and give me accolades on my abilities as a musician. I was beginning to get some serious recognition for my talents, and I liked it. I thought I had everything figured out and would finish every weekend, thinking I had given everything I had in the tank to the Lord through my excellent performance.

A few years into our time in the Tampa Bay area, the job market started to decline. I worked for several companies consecutively, which were eventually bought out and closed down. Finding work became increasingly challenging. Fortunately, an opportunity arose for me to regain my security clearance, which I knew would open up numerous job prospects with the government. However, it meant relocating, a tough decision given our strong ties to family, friends, and church.

In March of 2010, we ultimately decided to move. I anticipated it would take a year or two to regain the clearance and promised Sandra that we would return home once I secured it. Before leaving, I met with the worship team at our church and expressed my intention to take the lessons and experiences I had gained there with me and replicate them elsewhere. Looking back, it turned out to be one of the most unknowing statements I have ever made, as I had no idea what God had in store for our lives. And so, we embarked on our journey to Charleston, South Carolina.

I went ahead first so the kids could complete the school year, but after about a month, we all missed each other so much that we decided to commit and move the entire family. When the family arrived in our new location, Sandra and I felt it was essential to get involved in a church as soon as possible to make some friends. We initially tried a few larger churches, similar to the one we left behind, but couldn't establish a meaningful connection. Disheartened, we explored different options and enrolled the kids in tumbling classes at a local gymnastics center to keep them engaged.

On our first visit to the gym, we encountered a friendly hippie couple in the lobby. The husband sported a long ZZ Top–style beard, and the wife had long hair adorned with flowers and a floral dress, and both wore Jesus sandals. We noted them but didn't think much of it other than finding it pretty cool. On that day, I was wearing a black Zildjian cymbal T-shirt. A few minutes later, the man turned to me and said, "Hey, I like your shirt. Are you a musician?" I replied, "Yes, I am," and it sparked a conversation. He inquired about the type of music I played and where I performed. I explained that I was a worship musician, and we had just moved to the area and were looking for a church.

To my surprise, despite his unconventional appearance, he smiled and said, "Really? I'd like to invite you to our church. It's called the River Church, just up the road." He informed us that it was a recently established church that met in a local elementary school. Intrigued, we decided to check it out that Sunday. We felt so welcomed as soon as we walked in that we decided to make it our regular church. The man, whom I affectionately referred to as the "hippie man" who had invited us, was named Steven and was the pastor of discipleship. He had a genuine passion for his calling. He introduced me to the works of Francis Schaeffer and Ravi Zacharias and an impressive list of authors who significantly impacted my spiritual journey.

Steven was an extraordinary guitarist, a true virtuoso, but our conversations went far beyond music. He didn't even play guitar with the worship team on Sunday mornings. While I came in with the preconceived notion that I would bring all I had learned from the churches back home to our new location, God had different plans. He transformed my perspective. Pastor Steven embraced me as I was, recognized my potential, and became the first person to see me as more than just a talented kid. He saw me as a man, engaged in conversations with me like a man, and challenged me as a real man should be challenged. Until then, being a musician had been my primary identity and how I defined myself. Even as a husband, father, and military man, I primarily saw myself as a musician. Steven's challenges ignited a longing for something more profound within me. It initiated a journey of self-discovery. I began to desire recognition as more than a talented musician. I longed for someone to acknowledge not only me but specifically the Christ within me, much like Pastor Steven had done.

Remarkably, the security clearance paperwork returned in just a few months, which was nothing short of divine intervention since the typical waiting time for these investigations often exceeded a year or more. Coupled with our overwhelming homesickness and my promise to Sandra, stating that I would take her back once the clearance was granted, I updated my résumé and uploaded it to a few job websites. Within approximately a week, I received a job offer that offered a higher salary than anything we had ever encountered in Tampa. The job was as a contractor for US Central Command at MacDill AFB. Consequently, in July 2010, we returned to our hometown near Tampa with a new spark and a fresh perspective on God.

I took the position of senior systems engineer as a subcontractor to Microsoft on an IT support contract. A few months later, I was promoted to technical project manager to oversee the construction of a new headquarters building. My job was overseeing the project to build and migrate all systems and applications from the old data center to the new one. It was a *big* job…I averaged sixty-five hours or more a week for a few years, and once the project was done, I was promoted to lead messaging architect for the entire command. This was an *even bigger* job. I worked full day-shift hours in Tampa, with an area of responsibility (AOR) in the Middle East. I had to be available twenty-four-seven. It was very taxing on my sleep, health, and family. After some time, Sandra pulled me aside and said, "Honey, something has got to change." She could see it was killing me and that it was affecting the whole family. It was a hard decision for me to leave because I had progressed into a senior management role and had oversight of some of the most critical systems in the most active command in the military. It was the real deal. At this point, I believed, like many men, that my profession was my identity.

In seeking wisdom from the Lord, I realized how much my family and I needed a work-life balance. I submitted my résumé to a few job sites and received a job offer from a small government contracting company closer to home. I was familiar with the company and had talked to them a year or so prior about a different position on one of their contracts that they had just won, but it was in the process of being contested at the time and was too much of a risk for me. This time, they had an opening on the corporate side and were looking for a senior system engineer to manage the corporate network. I went through a lengthy interview process and was offered a job, and the commute to the office was a dream commute. We took a pretty substantial pay cut, but at that point, money was not as important to us as it was to stabilize the family.

Six months into my employment, a significant event occurred, and my boss was let go. I was asked if I wanted a promotion to director of the department. Already feeling that our family was healing well, I accepted the offer, and the raise was more than I ever made during all those complicated and trying years at US Central Command. The Lord had proven how good he is once again. I am happy to say that as of the time this was written, I am still working with the same organization and that my work-life balance is indescribable.

When we returned home from Charleston, we returned to the big church we attended when we moved away. We tried for a few months to reconnect but were struggling. I used to think it had changed too much over the few months we were away, but I now realize we had changed. The Lord had made us aware of something, but we couldn't put our finger on it just yet. We started noticing a change in our oldest daughter, Dana. We would take her and drop her off at the youth group, and she was having difficulty connecting because it had grown very large (more than fifteen hundred kids). When we asked her if she wanted to go, she would say no and act strangely. Other factors weighed into the decision. I won't go into it because I am not trying to imply anything was wrong with the church. We were changing, so it no longer seemed the right fit.

Sandra's parents were going to a church just a few minutes up the road from our house, and we had some friends there and tried it a few times. It was quite different and took a while for us to get used to, but our kids connected very well. Our oldest daughter, Dana, was excited about attending the youth group. I was getting involved in the tech team and worship teams. Sandra was making very close friends. It was a good fit. We began attending regularly in April 2011. We grew in our identity there. For me, it started, as it always does, in the worship team. I also started using my technical skills by helping the tech team.

The interesting thing is that up to this point, there had never been an overlap. I always worked a very technical job to support my family. Still, I never used those skills in any of the churches I had attended, other than running sound on occasion or helping set up a "church in the box" sound system at the church in Charleston. I took to this full steam and found joy in building the tech team infrastructure, eventually taking over the whole tech ministry. It was an exciting time because I managed the tech team while still being an active worship team member. I was now seen as more than just a musician, and I loved it.

Throughout the next few years, I was asked if I would be interested in observing the elder board. I spent a few months attending these meetings as a fly on the wall, watching and listening. I was unsure why I was allowed to be in the room. Then, one day, I was told thanks for attending these meetings. I was told they were having a meeting that night but said that I didn't need to be there, as they had some private meetings scheduled that only the elders could attend. It sounded good, and I didn't think much about it. The following month, the same thing happened, and the same happened the next month. Then I was asked to return to the meetings, so I thought, "Sure, why not?" When I walked in this time, though, they had me sit at the table with them instead of off to the side like before. I was shocked when I realized what was going on. I was being considered for eldership in the house. What? I was being interviewed by the men I had been observing and for whom I had gained immense respect. What was I doing here? How did I get here? Every aspect of my life was changing, and I was becoming elevated to leadership in every area of my life. Family, work, tech ministry, worship ministry, and now I am sitting here being considered for this honor. I was still in my thirties and at least twenty years younger than everyone in that room.

The interview process was very encouraging. At the next meeting, they asked if I would bring Sandra so that they could interview and evaluate us as a married couple. They told us they had witnessed our faithful servanthood in the house. They saw how we walked together as husband and wife and how we loved and parented our children. They spoke to the leadership qualities that we had demonstrated within the church. A week or so later, we were confirmed by the board. The elder board called out identity over us and said I was now an elder in the church body. It was so overwhelming then, and I told them I didn't know if I wanted this and said I would have to pray about it. That was when the pastor looked me in the eyes like he was staring directly into my soul and said, "That is how we know that you are ready and have been called and elevated to this position in the kingdom." I served the board faithfully for several years, observing how God moves through his people.

During this time, I was introduced to a new ministry event. Our pastor wanted all the elders to go through this three-day Fully Alive retreat focused on spiritual healing. I hesitated to say yes because I didn't feel like I needed anything addressed then and only went out of obedience. I am so glad I went because it was a powerful experience and was the first time I had witnessed a ministry like this. I witnessed some of the biggest and most formidable men I'd ever seen break down in tears and completely surrender their hearts to the Lord as he moved to break down strongholds in their lives. It was also the first time in all my years in ministry that I learned that I was a child of God and that I should guard my heart. It gave me a toolbox of ministry tools I have used a lot over the years.

In the years to come, a series of events led to some hard times, and the enemy was causing friction in the church. I cannot provide details out of love and respect for all involved, but I can say that the Lord elevated me to that position for a particular purpose and time. I have only recently gained this understanding from the Lord. My purpose was to be the moderator of the men on that board; I was the person the Lord charged with maintaining integrity throughout a difficult and painful process. I also know there was a wake of hurt left behind that God has not only mended, but he has also exponentially blessed the relationships of all the individuals involved.

As I reflected back on that time, the Lord brought me to the passage James 1:12: "Blessed is a man who perseveres under trial; for once he has been approved, he will receive the crown of life, which the Lord has promised to those who love him." I can sit here now and write about the experience with peace from the Father above that I did well in his sight, but I could not see it then.

In 2018, the long and challenging process that the church went through was resolved, and the Lord called us elsewhere. We were unsure where we were supposed to be. We only knew that our time there was done. A new church was being planted a few miles up the road in Apollo Beach, Florida, from resources entrusted to them by the church we were being called away from, and they had a significant need that we could meet.

I met with both pastors and shared with them where the Lord was leading us, and after clearing up a few things, I met with the pastor of our new church. We met for lunch, and before he said anything, I told him, "I never wanted to be an elder ever again." I could see that that statement visibly took him aback. He and I had served on that same elder board for several years. We talked for quite some time, and he could see that I was hurting, angry, and confused about what I was supposed to be doing and that I needed to be ministered to. He invited me to attend a new three-day retreat called Centurions that is focused on identity in Christ.

Like before, I said yes out of obedience to my pastor but honestly did not want to be there. As it happens, all the elders and pastors from the last church were attending the same event on the other side of the same property where I was with all the elders and pastors from the new church. This retreat had elements of healing similar to Fully Alive, which was good, as I had new hurts that needed to be addressed.

There was a moment during the retreat when I was so frustrated and angry over everything that had happened that it came out again during one of the ministry sessions. Once again, I told my pastor I never wanted to be an elder. My pastor, a close friend, looked me directly in the eye and calmly asked me, "Dustin, what hurts you so badly? I was witness to all that happened." He offered some words of encouragement directly to me and then said, "You have associated the hurt you experienced with the title of elder." He then asked if it was just the title or if there was more to it. I didn't know how to answer that. I just said I didn't know, and he told me to head to the woods and seek clarification from the Lord.

The extended time in the woods was good for me, and the Lord reminded me of the tools in my toolbox that I received during Fully Alive, and real healing took place. The Lord changed my perspective on life and ministry. Going in, I thought my identity was in being an elder and that it had all been taken away from me. I came out knowing only one thing: I was a child of God and was right where God wanted me to be.

A few weeks later, my pastor gave me a ministry license and called me Pastor Dustin. Tears just swelled, and my heart was softened so much because he found a way to show me that he saw the calling on my life. He saw Christ's calling for me and did it in a way I didn't want to reject. I have tried to serve as well as I can as a pastor, worship leader, technical director, and music director in the church.

Once again, the enemy attacked me in a manner I never saw coming. This time, though, the attack came at work. The company I have been working for became victim to a major ransomware cyberattack that significantly impacted the business. It took months to recover. As the head of the department, I had to bear the brunt of the blame. This was a very difficult experience for me, as I have always done my job with excellence.

Before this event, my pastor had set up a monthly pastoral council meeting where all the church's pastors would get together once a month for discipleship. I became so distracted with the recovery process at work and the fact that I had lost the confidence of the executive management team at my company that I kept missing the pastoral meetings. I started feeling like I was letting my pastor down, and eventually, I called him and said I was sorry, but I could no longer attend these meetings until I got everything stable again. I wasn't sure if I could get things normalized again or if I would have a job anymore. It was a stressful time. Eventually, we recovered operations, and I did not lose my job. I took a reputation hit to my career with my company, which was a hard pill to swallow.

I began to hear the enemy speaking lies to me. He told me I was only asked to be a pastor to appease me. He told me I wasn't worthy of the title, and I started to believe it. He was, however, unsuccessful in trying to convince me that I was not worthy of being a child of God. At the time, I decided not to return to being a part of the pastoral council.

It's been a few years since that event. We have continued to serve faithfully in the church. Our middle daughter, Leah, married the pastor's son and is now the worship leader at the church, and I am the music director.

It has always been a dream of mine to have land to build a homestead. In 2022, the dream became a reality for us, and we sold our home and purchased a seven-acre property. The property is tucked into a wooded area a few miles out of the congestion of town with a beautiful creek that splits the middle of the property, a large move-in-ready home, and a few outbuildings for my workshop and storage. Having this space has been such a tremendous blessing to our family. We have had so much fun together working the land, carving paths through the woods, planting fruit trees, building gardens, and raising chickens. Before this, I had encountered the presence of God the most, alone in the quietness of the woods of my retreat experiences, and now he gave me my own woods to be alone with him whenever I wanted. Praise God.

A few months into the new property, I got a call from my dad. He said he was getting kicked out of the place he had been staying over a disagreement with his landlord and that he had no place to go. I did not want him to be homeless, but I also knew that my dad had a horrible temper. I was hesitant to let him come and live on the property with us. We had a good relationship growing up, but as he had gotten older, the relationship had become strained because of some poor decisions and an occasional narcissistic personality.

I had years of pent-up frustration, and I did not want to allow him to move onto the property because we needed to maintain distance to coexist at this point in life. I knew that having him there might not be healthy for our relationship, and I felt he had no respect for boundaries. In addition, his poor decisions were starting to have a significant and direct financial impact on my household, as we had loaned him a considerable amount of money to help him recover after he fell victim to a financial scam that robbed him of his life savings. It was causing severe dissension and bitterness in my heart.

I talked through options with Sandra, and we decided to purchase an RV for him to stay in on the property and have him pay us rent. However, we failed to address the required boundaries adequately. We continued to see evidence of poor decisions and caught him in several lies, trying to cover up or blame someone else for his poor choices. Eventually, there was a huge blow-up in front of my family. It was a shameful moment in my life, and I deeply regret the events of that night.

When my dad gets angry, there is a switch that flips inside of him, and it is like a demonic spirit comes upon him. When this happens, he is entirely unable to calm down. My sister and I can see in his eyes that it is no longer our dad, but something else is controlling him. This particular night, our tempers got the best of us, leading to a huge fight. I don't want to go into the full details of the night, as it is very personal. Still, I will say that night, my father said something I interpreted as very disrespectful to me in front of my wife and kids, and I completely lost my temper and stood up to him like I never had before. As I was yelling for him to get out of my house, I felt the Lord impressing on my heart that if I didn't stop, the demonic spirit of anger that was upon him was going to be transferred to me and be mine to carry. This is not a proud moment in my life. However, it brought awareness of the generational curses that needed to be broken so they were not further passed down my family tree.

As I mentioned, my journey toward creating an intentional legacy began at forty-seven. The idea to be intentional came from an unexpected source: social media—in particular, a friend's comment about me on a social media post. I don't recall what the original post was about, but I was in a picture someone had tagged me in. When I saw it, I read through the comments, and my dear friend Alejo, whom I connect with on so many levels, commented, "Any man can be a teacher or a pastor, but not every man can father as Dustin does."

That comment spoke to me in so many ways. It connected with my spirit, and I knew it was what the Lord called me to be; it was my real identity. Not only had I been fathering my children, but also the employees who work for me and the ministries that the Lord made me a part of. It really pulled at my heartstrings. I knew it was my real calling, my real identity.

Being a military man, I understand the importance of rank and the chain of command. Having worked in the corporate world for as long as I have, I know how important titles are in career progression. Being in church my whole life, I know the significance of eldership in the church and the burden that being a pastor carries. My road to discovering my real identity took me through the rise and fall of every title we hold on to as men. However, none of these titles or positions ever had the impact on me that being called a good father did.

A few months later, I attended the funeral of a lifelong friend. His children were very good friends of Sandra's and mine in our youth group years. I was in tears throughout the entire memorial service. Yes, I was saddened by the loss of my friend, but what had me in tears was the way his family and friends talked about him. They truly honored him. His oldest daughter came up and spoke about her daddy, and as she did, she had a slideshow playing in the background with pictures of each of his kids and grandkids. She shared how each of them had a little piece of her daddy in them and spoke not just to him as a man but to Christ and the love that he displayed. It was so touching, and I cried because that is precisely what I want my kids to say about me when I am called home into eternity. I am not fearful about death because I know where I will spend my eternity, but I have always been saddened at the thought of not being there for my family.

I posted this thought on Facebook after the memorial service, and his oldest daughter replied to my post and told me that the very fact that I felt that way meant that I was well on the path. I felt like my heart stopped at that moment. I chose to be intentional from that moment forward but didn't know how to do it. Sure, I knew I would show more love to all of them. But I knew if I was going to be an influential fatherly figure to my family, friends, and ministries, I needed to seek advice from the original Father who created the greatest legacy of all time.

And so, my quest began. I had so much on my mind…

The Lord opened up a door to attend a retreat called Quest. This retreat was six days long instead of three days like the previous retreats I had participated in. I was familiar with it, as in I knew of its existence, and I also knew that my earlier retreat experiences would not have been possible had the authors not attended Quest. It was at this very retreat where God inspired them to write their impactful ministries. Coincidentally, going into this retreat, I again had some significant hurts and anger in my heart toward my dad. In addition, Sandra and I were butting heads on everything from money to intimacy. I had become so frustrated with work and worship that I did everything possible to stay as busy as possible and take my mind off everything. I needed something, and I needed it now. I jumped at the opportunity to attend this retreat, and for the first time, I wasn't going out of obedience to my pastor. I was seeking it and going because I needed it.

I knew the enemy had been attacking my very identity and was trying to stop me from progressing into what I was called to be. The first day, I walked into the woods until I found a peaceful river running through the property. I sat my chair in the shallow water facing the rising sun, took off my shoes, stuck my feet in the brisk water, and started my first devotional. After I finished, I closed my eyes and sat silently as the sun rose and started shining on my face. I resisted the urge to open my eyes and heard rustling in the water before me. As I was sitting there, I started to listen to this quiet voice from deep inside, challenging me. It said, *What are you here for? Are you just going to dip your toes in this water? Or are you all in?*

Splash! I was floating down the river.

I found what I needed. I needed the Lord, and I found him. I am grateful that the Lord opened the door for me to attend. If I could describe the experience, I would say it was quiet, purposeful, powerful, and inspirational. The Lord gave me a clear vision, gave me purpose, and provided me with the inspiration to write this book. I left there with peace in my heart, having passed all my hurts, concerns, and sins to the Lord, wanting him more than ever.

- He set me on a quest to seek him passionately with all my heart, every day.
- He gave me the tools to know how to seek healing.
- He gave me the identity to move forward because I will fall back to my past hurts without it.
- He showed me the importance of the journey and how to build a purposeful, Godly legacy.

After the retreat, my pastor wanted to meet and discuss my experience. It was the most open, honest, sincere, and easy conversation I had ever had with him. I shared my retreat experience and told him all that the Lord revealed to me, including the vision of this book. He encouraged me to keep writing and questing after the Lord. I apologized for my closed-mindedness toward the eldership and pastorship and told him that the Lord called me to father the ministries I am involved in, regardless of titles.

For the first time, I truly understood what being an elder and a pastor meant. The Lord had called me to be a father in all aspects of my life. I told him that I was willing and open to serve in whatever capacity the Lord called me into, wherever there was a need. A few months later, I received word that I was being invited back into the pastoral counsel, and this time, I knew in my heart what that meant.

I pray that this book inspires you to be purposeful in living a Godly life—one that leaves a legacy so powerful that if Jesus spoke about you at your memorial service, he would say, "I know them well."

GODLY LEGACY

Godly legacy begins with Sonship. I know this book is written from a male perspective, particularly from a married and aged man's perspective. That is because God asked me to write about legacy from my viewpoint through the lenses of my experiences. I believe that every one of these principles can be applied to both men and women, whether you are married or divorced or have kids or not.

Isaiah 64:8 says, "We are the clay; you are the potter; we are all the work of your hand." Applying these principles into your life will allow the Father to mold you in his image and empower you to build an amazing legacy.

Sonship is the position of being a son, especially a son of God. Being his son or daughter, you now gain all the privileges and responsibilities of a child in God's family.

And 1 Peter 2:10 says that once we were not a people, but now you are God's people; you had not received mercy, but now you have received mercy.

What this passage is saying is that you are included in the family of God now that you have become a child of God. Your identity is no longer your profession, your talents, or abilities. Your identity becomes a child of God, and radical transformation takes place in your life, and you go from being lost to slaves to children to heirs. Here is what that means:

This new identity frees us:

- You once were a slave to the law, to sin with no rights or privileges. You were a slave completely controlled by a master. Ephesians 2:1–2 states, "And you were dead in your trespasses and sins in which you previously lived according to the ways of this world, according to the ruler of the power of the air, the spirit now working in the disobedient." Once you are a child of God, you receive all the rights and privileges belonging to that status.
- As you stood guilty before God, you were an object of wrath because of your enslavement to sin. Ephesians 2:3 states, "We too all previously lived among them in the fleshly desires, carrying out the inclinations of our flesh and thoughts, and we were by nature children under wrath as the others were also." As a child of God, you stand before him, reconciled, made holy, blameless, and free from accusation in Jesus Christ. The apostle Paul speaks to this in his letter to the Colossians. In chapter 1, verses 18–19, he writes that "Christ is head of the body, the church; he is the beginning, the firstborn from the dead, so that he might come to have first place in everything. For God was pleased to have all of his fullness dwell in him."
- Once dead, we are now alive in Christ. Ephesians 2:4–5 states, "But God, who is rich in mercy, because of his great love that he had for us, made us alive in Christ even though we were dead in trespasses. You are saved by Grace."

Through this identity, we are drawn into an intimate and personal relationship with God, where we have the identity, status, position, and heart of a son. This change in relationship is expressed in our prayer language, which becomes Christlike.

In the book of Mark, chapter 14, verse 36, we hear Jesus crying out to the Father in the garden, saying, "Abba, Father! All things are possible for you. Take this cup away from me. Nevertheless, not what I will, but what you will."

The term Abba is Aramaic for "Daddy" or "Father." Notice the way Jesus spoke in this passage. "Abba, Father!" I believe there was a moment of desperation in his voice when he cried out, "Abba," followed by a long pause where the weight of the world weighed down upon him. I believe he shouted, "Father! All things are possible for you; take this cup from me." I also think that in this moment, the Father looked down upon him and spoke identity, peace, and purpose to him. Therefore, Jesus submitted to the will of the Father and spoke the words: "Nevertheless, not what I will, but what you will."

Crying out "Abba, Father" is a prayer language filled with deep affection. It is a prayer that is deeply felt and intensely experienced, like a child crying out for his daddy.

Some of you reading this tend to have a more rational relationship with Jesus. I want to encourage you to give room for the Holy Spirit to move you into a more profound affection for an intense experience with God. It's OK for a man to be a crybaby. I know I am.

Sonship is knowing that you are a child of God. As I mentioned, every man will leave a legacy, but not every man will leave a biblically purposeful legacy.

When I first shared the introduction and journey section with my wife, she was quiet and then said it sounded like an autobiography about me. I chuckled a little bit because I had only given her a taste of what the Lord had given me. You might have been thinking the same thing while you were reading it, but I want to provide context into why this was important.

There is power in sharing our testimony. Through our testimony, people can relate to our stories and witness how the Lord worked through the process. They may be feeling helpless or hurting, or like there is nowhere to turn. When we share our testimony, particularly the parts where the Lord worked, it can offer hope to them that there is a light at the end of the tunnel.

On the last night of my Quest retreat, I had the opportunity to sit and talk with a couple of young men who were attending with me. These young men were starting on their journey of life. Both of them were in their early twenties and hungry for the Lord. We stayed up very late that night, getting to know each other by talking and sharing what the Lord was doing in our lives. At some point, I realized that I was doing most of the talking, and I paused for a minute to see if they had something to say. I apologized for being long-winded, but they both said no and told me to keep talking: "So much wisdom is being shared, and we want to hear it." This encouraged me to keep speaking to them. I felt like it may have been the first time that someone had spoken to them as men, and I knew how impactful that experience was for me. I began talking about identity, and one of them asked me, "What exactly do you mean by identity?"

I smiled and said, "I could tell you what it means, but it wouldn't be as impactful or relatable to you if I didn't share how I found my true identity in Christ." They both smiled and said, "Please share more so that we can better understand." I shared the same journey story with them that I shared with you, and when I was finished, one of the young men stood up and hugged me and said that he had never met anyone who could take something so profound and explain it in such a simple, relatable way. I could see the impact it had on him.

I do not take glory for that; it was all from the Lord. He used me as a facilitator to impart wisdom to those young men in that situation. He allowed me to work in accordance with my identity and father these two young men. I truly believe they will live extraordinary lives with a strong passion for pursuing the Lord and leave behind a robust and purposeful, Godly legacy. I hope the Lord will use me in an even greater capacity by providing the inspiration to complete this book. I pray that anyone who reads this will see the Christ at work in me and be inspired to build their own Godly legacy intentionally.

PRIORITIES

Prioritizing refers to the act of focusing on one thing over another, and it holds significant importance in the construction of a Godly legacy. Identifying and prioritizing critical elements in life is crucial as they form the groundwork for our legacy. For a Christian, the foremost priority is maintaining a close relationship with the Lord, making him the central focus and the highest priority in life.

> *For this reason, God highly exalted him and gave him the name that is above every name, so that at the name of Jesus every knee will bow—in heaven and on earth and under the earth—and every tongue will confess that Jesus Christ is Lord, to the glory of God the Father.*
> —Philippians 2:9–11

To put anything first in life is to hold something as a priority. We can determine our priorities based on where we devote most of our time and energy. If you want to be purposeful in building a Godly legacy, then you must prioritize your life to build a foundation deeply rooted in your faith in God. Putting God first means keeping him in mind when engaging with other people or activities.

- Priority 1: Your walk with Jesus
- Priority 2: Your spouse
- Priority 3: Your family
- Priority 4: Your work
- Priority 5: Your ministry

If any of these elements are out of order, the rest will suffer and crumble. Your legacy will not be as impactful, complete, or full of life as the Creator intended it to be.

A purpose-driven legacy means being very intentional about prioritizing what matters most in your life. Each priority is a building block for the next.

Our walk with Jesus should be personal. I know there are denominational differences at play, but the heart of a Godly legacy requires this first element to be built upon the solid foundation of our faith in Jesus. We must be consistent and steadfast in seeking him in every moment. The best way to do this is by staying in the Word and praying for direction.

Too many of us deify Jesus to the point that we don't pursue a personal relationship in the manner that God intended. Allow me to briefly expand on this statement and explain what it means and why it is so important.

The Apostle John addresses this in the gospel of John chapter 1: "In the beginning was the Word, and the Word was with God, and the Word was God" (1:1–3).

John 1:14 states, "And the word was made flesh, and took residence amongst us; we observed His glory, the glory of the One and Only Son from the Father."

John 1:17–18 states, "For although the law was given through Moses, grace and truth came through Jesus Christ. No one has ever seen God. The One and Only Son—the One who is at the Father's side—He has revealed Him."

John 14:25–26 states, "I have spoken these things to you while I remain with you. But the Counselor, the Holy Spirit, whom the Father will send in my name, will teach you all things and remind you of everything I have told you."

Let's connect the dots here. The first three verses state that the Word came first. It was with God…it was God…so God is the Word. Then, all of creation and history occur, and all the events of the Old Testament take place. Then, in verse 14 of this passage, it says the Word became flesh as the only Son of God. It does not say that the Word created another entity that was equal to God. It says that the *Word became God*. So Jesus is part of God.

So why am I saying this? Well, because God has a purpose and a plan. God gave Moses the law of the old covenant, and then he came through his Son Jesus to fulfill that law in order to make a new covenant with us through him. God became flesh through Jesus so that we could relate to him on a personal level so that we could witness and observe his nature in the flesh.

In John chapter 14, Jesus speaks of the third piece of God's plan. He tells us that God has given us the Holy Spirit, who will guide and counsel us. He does this through his Word, which was left behind for us in the Bible, our prayers and intercession, our worship, and our meditations.

When we call out in the name of something, we are told to call out in the name of Jesus. The Word says that when we do this, he will meet our needs so his Father can be glorified.

John 14:12–14 states, "Truly I tell you, the one who believes in me will also do the works that I do. And he will do even greater works than these, because I am going to the Father. Whatever you ask in my name, I will do it so that the Father may be glorified in the Son. If you ask me anything in my name, I will do it."

He knows things on a level that we can never fully comprehend, and the Word goes further to say that one day for us is like one thousand years for God. We can never fully comprehend all of God's plan or when it will be completed; we simply do not have the capacity for it. However, the Bible is the sufficient Word of God, meaning that it has more than enough of what we need to know to live in accordance with God's purpose and plan. It is the living, breathing Word of God, and spending time regularly in the word is the most crucial thing we can do in our relationship*s*. Notice that I highlighted the *s* at the end of the word relationship.

When we spend time in the word, God reveals his plan for us. The Holy Spirit guides and directs us to declare the name of Jesus over the situations in our lives so that he can act on our behalf and bring glory to the Father. We cannot enter into the kingdom of heaven without being covered by the blood of Jesus. That is why it is so important that Christ is evident in our legacy.

When people speak about you at your memorial service and speak to the Christ who was evident in your life, it means something. If they can see that in you, then the chances are good that God will see Jesus, who is a reflection of himself, when he looks at you on Judgment Day.

PRIORITY 1: YOUR WALK WITH JESUS

The key to building and leaving behind a Godly legacy is to live and walk a Godly life. The highest priority is being purposeful to have a consistent walk with Jesus.

"Walking with Jesus" is a metaphorical expression often used in Christian theology to describe a believer's personal relationship and spiritual journey with Jesus Christ. It goes beyond physical movement and implies a close, intimate companionship and alignment with Jesus's teachings and principles.

To walk with Jesus involves living by Christian values, following his moral teachings, and embodying his love, compassion, and humility daily. It signifies an ongoing, conscious effort to grow in faith, deepen one's understanding of the Scriptures, and maintain a continuous connection with God through prayer and devotion. In essence, walking with Jesus is a dynamic and transformative journey of faith, guided by the desire to emulate and follow the example set by Jesus Christ.

Keys to a Real and Personal Walk with the Lord

1. **Spend time in the word; make it a routine.** It may be hard at first, but in time, you will find that your heart desires more time with him each day. If you're unsure where to start, start in the Book of John and see where the Lord leads you, or pick up a devotional and read it daily to get you started. You will be surprised how often the Lord gives you precisely what you need in the moment.
2. **Spend time in prayer and intercession.** How should we pray? Well, the disciples asked Jesus the same thing, and his reply was this, in Matthew 6:9–13:

Therefore, you should pray like this: Our Father in heaven, your name be honored as holy. Your kingdom come. Your will be done on earth as it is in heaven. Give us today our daily bread. And forgive us our debts, as we also have forgiven our debtors. And do not bring us into temptation but deliver us from the evil one.

3. **Eliminate the distractions of life and meditate in silence, listening for a still, small voice to guide you.** For me, this means waking up before the rest of my family, sitting on the back patio with my Bible, and turning my phone off.
4. **Try and spend every moment with an awareness of God's presence.** We tend to spend countless hours focusing on things around us, unaware of the presence of God among us. Even further, we spend countless hours in church talking about Jesus without a single second of awareness of his presence in our midst. We must strive to be aware of his presence at every moment.
5. **Journal your time.** Write down what you hear and dream about. Then, take it to the Lord.

IDENTITY

When I started researching this subject, I opened my *Strong's Exhaustive Concordance of the Bible*. I was stunned when I found zero direct references in the KJV version of the Bible for the word *identity*. However, if you open any standard dictionary, you will find many different definitions.

One of the ways the dictionary defines identity is as the state or fact of remaining the same under varying aspects or conditions. [6] Fingerprints, for example, are unique to each person and are used by crime scene investigators to determine who committed a crime. These unique fingerprints are used to establish the identity of the perpetrator. Another way the dictionary defines identity is the condition or character as to who a person is, the qualities, beliefs, etcetera, that distinguish or identify a person or thing.

Each of us has a unique identity based on our individual characteristics, but we share the commonality that we are part of the human race.

What does it mean to have our identity in Christ? The Bible says that we are new creatures when we accept Jesus's sacrifice. We lose our identity and become pure, blameless, and forgiven. In this new identity, we become part of his body, where we are called to bless others in his name.

Wait a minute! How can that be? I thought you said there were no references in the Bible to identity!

I just meant that I could not find the direct term in the KJV concordance, but I assure you that identity is implied all through the scriptures. Let's take a look at a few…

There are thirteen books in the New Testament attributed to the apostle Paul. Paul begins each of his letters with a declaration of identity and purpose. Here are a few examples from the Bible.

---

6 "Identity Definition & Usage Examples." Dictionary.com. Accessed April 1, 2024. https://www.dictionary.com/browse/identity.

- Romans 1:1 Paul, a servant of Christ Jesus, called an apostle and set apart for the gospel of God.
- 1 Corinthians 1:1 Paul, called as an apostle of Christ Jesus by God's will.
- 2 Corinthians 1:1 Paul, an apostle of Christ Jesus by God's will.
- Galatians 1:1 Paul is an apostle—not from men or by man, but by Jesus Christ and God the Father, who raised him from the dead.
- Ephesians 1:1 Paul, an apostle of Christ Jesus by God's will: to the faithful saints in Christ Jesus.
- Philippians 1:1 Paul and Timothy, servants of Christ Jesus.
- Colossians 1:1 Paul, an apostle of Christ Jesus by God's will.

Most of us likely just read through this part and don't put too much thought into it, dismissing it as just a standard greeting of the day, but Paul had a purpose for each letter, and so he opened each letter with an introduction and declared:

I am Paul. God calls me to say this to you for this purpose. Wow! Now this is identity.

Whenever we experience an identity crisis, Scripture is a fantastic reminder that in him, we are chosen, and nothing can separate us from God's unconditional love.

Here are ten Bible verses about your identity that you should memorize and commit to heart.

1. 1 Peter 2:9: "But you are a chosen generation, a royal priesthood, a holy nation, His own special people, that you may proclaim the praises of Him who called you out of the darkness into His marvelous light."
2. 1 Corinthians 1:30: "But of Him you are in Christ Jesus, who became for us wisdom from God—and righteousness and sanctification and redemption."

3. 1 Peter 3:15: "But sanctify the Lord God in your hearts, and always be ready to give a defense to everyone who asks you a reason for the hope that is in you, with meekness and fear."
4. 1 Samuel 12:22: "For the Lord will not forsake His people, for His great name's sake, because it has pleased the Lord to make you His people."
5. Colossians 3:12: "Therefore, as the elect of God, holy and beloved, put on tender mercies, kindness, humility, meekness, longsuffering."
6. Ephesians 1:5: "Having predestined us to adoption as sons by Jesus Christ to Himself, according to the good pleasure of His will."
7. Ephesians 2:10: "For we are His workmanship, created in Christ Jesus for good works, which God prepared beforehand that we should walk in them."
8. Galatians 3:28: "There is neither Jew nor Greek, slave nor free, male nor female; for you are all one in Christ Jesus."
9. 1 John 3:1: "Behold what manner of love the Father has bestowed on us, that we should be called children of God! Therefore, the world does not know us because it did not know him."
10. 1 Corinthians 12:27: "Now you are the body of Christ, and members individually."

When we assume our rightful identity, the spirit of the Lord comes upon us. He anoints us to live a life of purpose. We become righteous trees that are deeply rooted with branches extending outward. As we grow and mature, we begin to produce sweeter and sweeter fruit.

> *The spirit of the Lord God is on me because the Lord has anointed me to bring good news to the poor. He has sent me to heal the brokenhearted, to proclaim liberty to the captives and freedom to the prisoners, to proclaim the year of the Lord's favor and the day*

of our God's vengeance; to comfort all who mourn, to provide for those who mourn in Zion; to give them a crown of beauty instead of ashes, festive oil instead of mourning and splendid clothes instead of despair. And they will be called righteous trees, planted by the Lord to glorify Him.
—Isaiah 61:1–4

The New International Version of this passage translates the term *righteous tree* as "oaks of righteousness."

I am an outdoors type of guy and live on a seven-acre homestead. I love the hard work that goes into maintaining the land and typically only come into the house to eat or sleep. When I think of the term "oaks of righteousness," I think of the large oak trees in my fields. One year, we had a hurricane hit our area head-on, and a tornado tore a line of destruction straight through a portion of our woods, taking out just about everything in its path. In total, we lost about thirty trees. Nearly every tree along the creek that runs through the middle of our property was uprooted and blown over, except for the oak trees. No oak tree was uprooted; the branches broke off or snapped down the middle, but they did not uproot. We spent a lot of time cleaning up afterward by cutting up the fallen trees and doing our best to save as many trees as possible. One of the trees we saved was a large oak tree, and the grandkids love to swing on it.

Sometime later, I decided to start taking out the stumps left behind to make it easier to mow the fields. As I began to dig out the stumps, I quickly realized how much deeper and broader the roots of the oak trees were than the maple trees. For the most part, I could dig the maple stumps out fairly easily with the backhoe on my small tractor, but the roots of the oak trees were tough to remove. I dug ten times deeper and ten times wider on each of them and still couldn't get them out. One day, I decided to burn one of the stumps, and after a few days, the stump finally turned to ash. A week later, I noticed smoke rising from the ground about twenty feet from the stump. When I dug it up to investigate, I found that the smoke was coming from the roots of an oak tree stump. The roots of an oak tree run very deep and very wide.

When we accept our identity in Christ, he plants us as oaks of righteousness into the fertile soil Jesus prepared for us. He showers us with the water of his grace. As we yearn for him, our identity takes root. We grow stronger while basking in the presence of the Holy Spirit. As we grow taller, we lean toward the direction of the Son, yearning for the radiant light that feeds us. As we mature in our identity, we begin to yield fruit that is sweeter and sweeter with age.

So what is required? How do we get there? When do I receive my identity?

The Bible gives us the formula; here it is. It is very simple. Are you ready?

1. **Acknowledge that you are a sinner.**
2. **Confess your sins to God. Ask God to forgive you of all your sins.**
3. **Ask God to come into your heart.**
4. **Accept Him as Lord and Savior of your life.**

It is cut-and-dried, and the Word says:

- Romans 3:23: "For all have sinned and fall short of the glory of God."
- Romans 6:23: "For the wages of sin is death, but the free gift of God is eternal life in Jesus Christ our Lord."
- Romans 5:8: "But God demonstrated His love towards us in that while we were yet sinners, Christ Jesus died for us."
- John 3:16: "For God so loved the world that, He gave his only

- begotten Son, that whosoever believes in Him should not perish, but have everlasting life."
- Ephesians 2:8: "For by Grace you have been saved through faith, and that not of ourselves, it is the gift of God."
- Romans 10:9–10: "That if you confess with your mouth Jesus as Lord, and believe in your heart that God raised Him from the dead, you will be saved; for with the heart a person believes, resulting in righteousness, and with the mouth he confesses, resulting in salvation."

My grandfather used to say that there is never a bad time for an altar call. I feel the same way, and if you have never truly accepted the Lord into your heart, I want to take a moment to pause right now and invite you to pray this simple prayer:

"Dear Lord Jesus, I know I am a sinner and ask for Your forgiveness. I believe you died for my sins and rose from the dead. I turn from my sins and invite you into my heart and life. I want to trust and follow you as my Lord and Savior. In your name. Amen."

If you just prayed this prayer for the first time, I want to be the first one to say welcome to the family. You are now officially called a "child of God." This is your new identity.

In Ephesians 2:8–10, Paul writes, "For by Grace you have been saved through faith. And this is not your own doing; it is the gift of God, not a result of works, so that no one may boast. For we are his workmanship, created in Christ Jesus for Good works, which God prepared beforehand, that we should walk in them."

As we start walking in this new identity, our hearts are made new, and we begin to do the good works. Make no mistake that works are required for salvation, but this passage makes it very clear that those works are Christ's works and not ours. Jesus completed the work and fulfilled all the laws of the Old Testament when he went to the cross.

Faith and acceptance of that fact is all that is required for our salvation and identity. Works are the demonstration of our faith. The more we seek the Lord, the more we desire to be like him. Through this process, our identity is enhanced and transformed as we mature in our faith.

HEALING AND RESTORATION

Accepting Christ and moving forward with your identity does not mean that there will be no pain or sorrow in your life. In fact, it may cause more pain and sorrow as God calls out the people and things that hinder your walk.

You may recall the offenses I shared in my journey testimony. Those were just a few of the many emotional hurts and offenses I have experienced. I assure you, like you, I have had many more over the years. I also know that I have hurt many people over the years, and those relationships can only be restored through the grace of God.

The Greek word for "heal" is *iaomai*, a verb that means to cure, make whole, be free from errors and sins, and bring about (one's) salvation.[7]

In Matthew 10:1, we see the authority Jesus gives us in his name: "Summoning his twelve disciples, he gave them authority over unclean spirits, to drive them out and to heal every disease and sickness."

This means that all authority in heaven has been given to us. In Jesus's name, we have the authority to intercede for healing, and if we have the faith to believe that he can do it, he will.

Notice the last part of the definition's references to sin. Healing is more than just physical and emotional; it is also spiritual. The last part of the Greek origin defines healing as being free from errors and sins

---

7 "IAOMAI Meaning - Greek Lexicon: New Testament (KJV)." Bible Study Tools. Accessed April 1, 2024. https://www.biblestudytools.com/lexicons/greek/kjv/iaomai.html#:~:text=Iaomai%20Definition,to%20bring%20about%20(one's)%20salvation.

to bring about (one's) salvation. In the simplest terms, sin is a transgression of God's spiritual law. It is something that we do in error that displeases the Lord.

I submit to you that all sin is equal in the eyes of God, as sin separates us from him. It drives a wedge between us and God. Obviously, the consequences of our sins are different in our world. The consequence of murder is much harsher than adultery in society. Suppose the murderer on death row earnestly confesses his sins to God and asks him for forgiveness. In that case, I do believe the Lord forgives and forgets that sin even if the family of the person he murdered does not, but he still has been convicted and has to face the consequences of his actions. I know that sounds controversial, but it is scripturally sound because God's grace is infinite and has no bounds.

> *And the God of all grace, who called you to his eternal glory in Christ, after you have suffered a little while, will himself restore you and make you strong, firm and steadfast.*
> —1 Peter 5:10

> *For all have sinned and fall short of the glory of God. They are justified through the redemption that is in Jesus Christ.*
> —Romans 3:23–24

If God is willing to forgive the murderer by his infinite grace, don't you think he would do the same for you? The good news is that he will…

Sometimes, God brings us to a mountaintop and meets us there, but we eventually have to come back down, and our faith will be tested. Knowing how to go before the Lord and confess our hurts and our sins is essential to building a Godly legacy.

The church I attended when I first became an elder would have a Wednesday night get-together on the first and third Wednesday of each month. The first Wednesday was an upper-room service and was a time of teaching and worship. The third Wednesday service was much lower-key and was set aside for elder prayer. On these nights, each of the elders would sit in pairs, and anyone who needed prayer would come and ask the elders to pray over them. There was usually a good turnout on both nights. The first time, I officially sat in the elder chair to pray. Someone from the worship team I knew well came to where I was sitting and asked for prayer. He and I had prayed several times in the past, but this time was very different. We prayed with him and interceded on behalf of the situation. When we finished, we hugged and prayed for the next person in line. As we finished, I noticed he was back in line again. He sat down and said, "I need you to pray again because I still feel the same way and need more prayer." So we interceded again, and the same thing happened. He came back for a third time. The other elder in my circle looked at me, and we were puzzled.

I realized then that this young man saw me in a different light now. He saw that I had been elevated in position within the church and wouldn't give up until I resolved his issue for him with my newfound authority. When he sat down again, I paused silently for a few minutes, waiting on the Lord. After a few moments, I looked him directly in the eyes and spoke. I told him that my only power and authority was through Jesus and that I wanted to pray again for him. I declared in the name of Jesus that he would give this young man the faith to believe that he could be healed. By this time, the rest of the elders had wrapped up their prayer time, had all joined our circle, and started praying the same thing over him.

He broke down in tears, embraced us all in a group hug, said thank you, and confirmed at that moment that he was indeed struggling with his faith and that it was directly impacting his ability to receive healing. The power in that moment wasn't in my position; it was in the power of the name of Jesus.

You have been given all the power and authority to declare the name of Jesus over your life, family, friends, church, and job. You have the authority to declare life in the name of Jesus. The name of Jesus is above all other names, and there is wonder-working power in the name of Jesus.

> *For this reason, God highly exalted him and gave him the name that is above every name, so that at the name of Jesus every knee will bow—In heaven and on earth—and every tongue will confess that Jesus Christ is Lord, to the glory of God the Father.*
> —Philippians 2:9–11

> *Truly I tell you, the one who believes in me will also do the works that I do. And he will do even greater works than these, because I am going to the Father. Whatever you ask in my name, I will do it so that the Father may be glorified in the Son. If you ask me anything in my name, I will do it.*
> —John 14:12–14

I am not a professional counselor or medical doctor, but if I were, I would tell you to put this in your toolbox and use it.

Let me give you a few more tools for your toolbox while I am at it.

God is a forgiving God. Psalm 103 is entitled "The Forgiving God." In verse 12, it says, "As far as the east is from the west, so far has he removed our transgressions from us."

Why east and west and not north and south? There is a reason for this. Have you ever heard of the East Pole or the West Pole? Of course, you haven't, and that is because they do not exist. The earth spins on a north-south axis. If you were to travel straight north, you would eventually reach the North Pole and start heading south until you reached the South Pole, and then you would be heading north again. These points are measurable. However, if you start going east, you will always face east. Same thing with a westerly direction. What this passage is saying is that when we confess our sins to the Lord, he casts them out of his memory. He casts them so far that they can never be found again.

This is a very important concept for us to grasp because we tend to confess our sins to the Lord and then hang onto them. If he can forget them, why can't we? Why do we dwell on our past hurts long after we have given them to God? That is a question I used to ask myself all the time. The reason that we keep looking back is that we have prioritized our hurts over our identity. Our identity is what keeps us moving forward with Christ.

> *The eye is the lamp of the body. If your eye is healthy, your whole body will be full of light. But if your eye is bad, your whole body will be full of darkness.*
> —Matthew 6:22–23

Shakespeare took inspiration from this passage when he wrote, "The eyes are the window to your soul." [8]

I have this thing I do now, and you might think I'm crazy, but it works for me. I figure that if the eyes are indeed the windows to the soul, doesn't it make sense that if I stare into my own eyes in the mirror long enough, I could see my soul and connect to it? I often find myself doing this in the morning as I get ready for the day, wondering if I will like what I see. Do I see Jesus carrying me or dancing with my soul?

This serves as a powerful and clear illustration for me. Visual representation is proven to be an effective tool for healing. When we confess our sins to the Lord, it is considerably easier for us to comprehend and process what we can see. Here is a simple example of what I mean.

---

[8] "Eyes Are Windows to the Soul - Bible Verses and the Biblical Meaning of Eyes." Bible Study Tools. Accessed April 1, 2024. https://www.biblestudytools.com/topical-verses/eyes-are-windows-to-the-soul-bible-verses/.

Take out a piece of paper, and spend some time with the Lord. Ask him to reveal the sins in your life hindering you from walking in the fullness of his glory. Ask him why you are mad or sick or whatever you need to ask. Whatever he reveals to you in this time, write it all down. Don't skip anything; be honest with yourself. Cuss, fight, do whatever it takes to get it all on paper. Use as many sheets of paper as you need to capture everything on your heart that you want to give to the Lord. Once you have everything written out, confess these things to him. Sit in silence for as long as it takes to feel the peace he brings you. Once you start feeling the serenity, burn everything you wrote down, and watch the words disappear. Then, spend some time thanking him and meditating in silence. When our eyes see our confessions burning away, our soul finds peace, and we remember that we gave this to the Lord, and now we can forget them too.

Another excellent tool for healing is transference and acting as a proxy.

A few years back, I got a call from a friend who had been fighting with his son. This fight got very personal, and the son yelled at him, "You're not my real dad; I don't need to listen to you." The father was very hurt because he adopted him at a very young age when he married his mother. He was desperate and asking for advice and prayer. I told him I would be right over, but while driving, the Lord told me to pick up his son and take him to the batting cages. When I arrived at the door, I could hear them yelling and screaming at each other. I knocked on the door, and when they opened it, I looked at the son and said, "Hey, buddy, why don't you come with me for a bit and get out of the house?" I looked at my friend, and we nodded in man code at each other.

While driving the son to the batting cages, I listened to his rant about the fight with his dad. When we got to the batting cages, I told him, "Here is what we are going to do." I picked up a bat and dropped a token into the machine, and as the balls came at me, I yelled out, "Dad!" and hit the ball as hard as I could. With the next ball, I said something else until all the balls were gone. He was laughing as he watched me do this. When my token expired, I handed him the bat and said, "Your turn." I spent quite a few tokens as he screamed word after word and smashed the balls as hard as he could.

When he got tired, he looked at me with tears in his eyes and said, "I think I need to go home now." So we got back into the car, and I drove him home. When he opened the door and saw his dad sitting there waiting on us, he broke down in tears, went running to him, and told him he was so sorry and that he didn't mean any of the things he said to him. The dad smiled and said, "Son, I forgive you," and I left so they could have their moment.

In this example, the son was able to take out all his frustration on something else. He was able to release all the anger that was built up inside. He was able to transfer all his anger out of his system by hitting an object. The anger was a distraction in his heart and mind, and once it was released, he could hear the voice of God speaking to him and telling him that he needed to make up with his dad.

A proxy works similarly. Sometimes, a person needs to get something out of their system, and they need someone to sit there and represent the person that hurt them so they can tell them precisely what is on their heart. It is important that if you choose to be a proxy, you cast no stones or try fixing the situation yourself. It is best to sit, listen, acknowledge, and apologize to them about what happened and then let the Lord work on their hearts in silence. We tend to overtalk and minister, sometimes thinking what we have to say is more important than what the Lord wants to say in the silence. Someone needed to hear that; I know I did.

Our Heavenly Father is always there, speaking to us. To hear him, we must eliminate the distractions in our lives. He is always available and willing to forgive and heal us if we have faith: "Indeed, the Protector of Israel does not slumber or sleep. The Lord protects you: the Lord is a shelter right by your side" (Ps. 121:4–5).

As you read through the New Testament accounts of the miracles Jesus performed, you see that he did this in many different ways. In some instances, he said, "Rise and sin no more"; in others, he said, "It was because of your faith that you were healed."

- John 5:1–16: "After this, a Jewish festival took place, and Jesus went up to Jerusalem. By the Sheep Gate in Jerusalem there is a pool, called Bethesda in Aramaic, which has five colonnades. Within these lay a large number of the disabled—blind, lame, and paralyzed. One man was there who had been disabled for thirty-eight years. When Jesus saw him lying there and realized he had already been there a long time, he said to him, 'Do you want to get well?' 'Sir,' the disabled man answered, 'I have no one to put me into the pool when the water is stirred up, but while I'm coming, someone goes down ahead of me.' 'Get up,' Jesus told him, 'pick up your mat and walk.' Instantly, the man got well, picked up his mat, and started to walk. Now that day was the Sabbath, and so the Jews said to the man who had been healed, 'This is the Sabbath. The law prohibits you from picking up your mat.' He replied, 'The man who made me well told me, "Pick up your mat and walk."' 'Who is this man who told you, "Pick up your mat and walk"?' they asked. But the man who was healed did not know who it was because Jesus had slipped away into the crowd that was there. After this, Jesus found him in the temple and said to him, 'See, you are well. Do not sin anymore, so that something worse doesn't happen to you.' The man went and reported to the Jews that it was Jesus who had made him well. Therefore, the Jews began persecuting Jesus because he was doing these things on the Sabbath."
- Luke 8:42–48: "While he was going, the crowds were nearly crushing him. A woman suffering from bleeding for twelve

years, who had spent all she had on doctors and yet could not be healed by any, approached from behind and touched the end of his robe. Instantly her bleeding stopped. 'Who touched me?' Jesus asked. When they all denied it, Peter said, 'Master, the crowds are hemming you in and pressing against you.' 'Someone did touch me,' said Jesus. 'I know that power has gone out from me.' When the woman saw that she was discovered, she came trembling and fell down before him. In the presence of all the people, she declared the reason she had touched him and how she was instantly healed. 'Daughter,' he said to her, 'your faith has saved you. Go in peace.'"

- Matthew 8:5–13: "When he entered Capernaum, a centurion came to him, pleading with him, 'Lord, my servant is lying at home paralyzed, in terrible agony.' He said to him, 'Am I to come and heal him?' 'Lord,' the centurion replied, 'I am not worthy to have you come under my roof. But just say the word, and my servant will be healed. For I too am a man under authority, having soldiers under my command. I say to this one, "Go," and he goes; and to another, "Come," and he comes; and to my servant, "Do this!" and he does it.' Hearing this, Jesus was amazed and said to those following him, 'Truly I tell you, I have not found anyone in Israel with so great a faith. I tell you that many will come from east and west to share the banquet with Abraham, Isaac, and Jacob in the kingdom of heaven. But the sons of the kingdom will be thrown into the outer darkness where there will be weeping and gnashing of teeth.' Then Jesus told the centurion, 'Go. As you have believed, let it be done for you.' And his servant was healed that very moment."

Sometimes, healing means we must confess our sins and ask for forgiveness; other times, it means we need more faith. Confessing our sins is an act of faith because we are saying, "Lord, I give this to you; please take it from me so that I may be healed."

If you don't believe the Lord can and will do this for you, then maybe your faith is not strong enough to receive the healing, and you need to pray for the faith to believe you can be healed.

Let's take the Pharisee Nicodemus, a great teacher who was astounded at what Jesus did as an example. Nicodemus requested a private and personal meeting with Jesus to ask him some questions weighing on his heart after witnessing the results of a miracle that Jesus performed after he had failed while attempting the same thing.

John 3:9–12 states, "'How can these things be?' asked Nicodemus. 'Are you a teacher of Israel and don't know these things?' Jesus replied. 'Truly I tell you, we speak what we know and we testify to what we have seen, but you do not accept our testimony. If I have told you about earthly things and you don't believe, how will you believe if I tell you about heavenly things?'"

Maybe you need to spend some more time in the Word with the Lord. He is ready to hear you, heal you, forgive you, and forget your trespasses. Are you ready to be like him?

THE BLUF

One of the terms frequently used in the military is "Give me BLUF: The Bottom Line Up Front." Each briefing would have a BLUF statement right at the beginning, and everything else was supporting documentation to support the BLUF. So here is the BLUF to wrap up this section.

Our personal relationship with God is the bedrock foundation upon which our legacy is built. He gives us an identity and a purpose that is only discovered when we prioritize him over ourselves. Our identity in Christ is of the utmost importance because it directs us to keep moving forward. There will be additional pain and hurts throughout our lives, but when we know how to forgive, forget, and seek him for healing, we must look to our identity so that we do not revert to our old sinful ways.

Keep on seeking him daily. Quest after him with all your heart. The more you do, the more meaningful your legacy will be.

Priority 1: Your Walk with Jesus: Reflection and Application

1. At the beginning of each week, write down one or two things that matter to you and God. Examples: spending time with God, having a strong marriage, understanding each of your children.
2. Are you thinking more and more of heaven and being with the Lord Jesus?
3. Remember you were created for a purpose. Take some time to meditate in the presence of the Lord, and ask him to reveal his call on your life.
4. Absorb the fact that time is short. You are just passing through this world. How can we intentionally make time for God?
5. Take time to write or record your spiritual journey—your childhood memories about faith, your salvation experience, what lessons God has taught you, etcetera.

PRIORITY 2: YOUR SPOUSE

Your essence. The pivotal aspect of your being is your heart, serving as the epicenter where the "real you" resides. Proverbs 27:19 observes, "The heart of man reflects man," emphasizing the profound influence of the heart on one's character. In line with Proverbs 23:7, which states that "as a person thinks in his heart, so is he," the significance of the heart in shaping one's identity is underscored.

Your core. Given that the physical heart is positioned at the center of your body, pumping life-sustaining blood to every living cell, the term "heart" has been employed for centuries to denote the fundamental origin of your thoughts, beliefs, values, motives, and convictions.

Your central command. Your heart functions as the Pentagon of your operations, profoundly impacting every facet of your life. Consequently, the direction of your heart plays a pivotal role in influencing all areas of your existence.

That is why the highest priority in building a biblical legacy is your relationship with the Heavenly Father. It is the very foundation that all else is built upon.

We associate love with the heart, and the "real you" was never meant to be alone. It was meant to love and to be loved.

After God had created the garden and put a man in charge, he said:

> Then the Lord God said, "It is not good for the man to be alone. I will make a helper corresponding to him." The Lord God formed out of the ground every wild animal and every bird of the sky and brought each to the man to see what he would call it. And whatever the man called a living creature, that was its name. The man gave names to all the livestock, to the birds of the sky, and to every wild animal; but for the man no helper was found corresponding to him. So the Lord God caused a deep sleep to come over the man, and he slept. God took one of his ribs and closed the flesh at that place. Then the Lord God made the rib he had taken from the man into a woman and brought her to the man. And the man said: This one, at last, is bone of my bone and flesh of my flesh; this one will be called "woman," for she was taken from man. This is why a man leaves his father and mother and bonds with his wife, and they become one flesh. Both the man and his wife were naked yet felt no shame. (Gen. 2:18–25)

In Matthew 19, Jesus departed from Galilee and went to the region of Judea, where large crowds followed him, and he healed people there. The story says that some Pharisees approached him to test him. They asked him, "Is it lawful for a man to divorce his wife on any grounds?" In verses 4 through 6, Jesus replied, "Haven't you read that he who created them, in the beginning, made them male and female, and he also said 'For this reason, a man will leave his father and mother and be joined to his wife, and the two will become one flesh. Therefore, what God has joined together, let no one separate.'"

One flesh! When a man and woman are joined in holy matrimony, there is a private and intimate moment between them that follows, during which the man goes into the woman and consummates the marriage vows, and they are joined as one flesh.

For this very reason, it is essential that you prioritize your spouse over everything else.

While attending my Quest retreat, I talked to some other guys at lunch and asked them if they had ever seen the movie *Fireproof*, with Kirk Cameron.[9] Coming into the retreat, I felt like Sandra and I were at each other's throats about anything and everything. We were arguing about everything from finances to intimacy and were both starting to get the urge to cut loose and run. As the Lord drew me in and revealed things to me, it hit me that we had been married for over twenty-six years and that I had never given her my whole heart. I had never prioritized her the way I should have. I had always prioritized myself over her. As I was sitting around the lunch table talking to the guys, I asked them for the name of the accompanying book and said that I wanted to give that a try; two of the men I was talking with smiled and said that they had both done the Love Dare challenge on their wives and that it worked. They said that the message of this story was a perfect illustration of what happens when our priorities are out of order.

If you haven't seen the movie, it is the story of a man who did not prioritize his wife until it was almost too late. The film is about a married couple, Caleb, a fire captain, and Catherine Holt, a hospital administrator, experiencing marital difficulties. At work, Caleb underscores the importance of never leaving one's partner behind, but he and Catherine argue constantly at home. Catherine accuses Caleb of being selfish because he prioritizes his desire for an unnecessary and expensive boat and leaves her to consider paying for needed medical equipment for Catherine's ailing mother. She is also frustrated about his habitual use of internet pornography and his leaving her to handle all the home responsibilities and overheads herself. Caleb feels attacked. Their constant arguing escalates

---

9 "Fireproof (Film)." Wikipedia, February 18, 2024. https://en.wikipedia.org/wiki/Fireproof_(film).

to the point where Caleb loses his temper and lashes out. Consequently, Catherine wants a divorce, to which an enraged Caleb agrees.

Caleb's best friend and fellow firefighter, Michael, and his father, John, convince him to hold off on divorce proceedings. His father persuades him to try the Love Dare, a forty-day challenge for marriage improvement in which a spouse alters how they treat their partner. Caleb reluctantly agrees, though he decides not to tell Catherine. Catherine has been openly flirting with Dr. Gavin Keller at the hospital where she works.

Caleb begins the Love Dare halfheartedly, viewing the tasks as more of a checklist than mutual outreach. Meanwhile, nurses at Catherine's hospital warn her not to trust Caleb, as they believe he is trying to butter her up to secure a more favorable divorce settlement. With encouragement from his father and Michael, Caleb continues, though Catherine eschews his affections and grows closer to Dr. Keller. Finding Catherine unmoved, Caleb is consoled by his father, while Michael reveals that he was divorced before marrying his current wife. Caleb sustains burns on the job, is admitted to the hospital where his wife works, and is treated by Dr. Keller. During treatment, Dr. Keller discovers that Catherine is married to Caleb but continues his affections. With renewed faith, Caleb continues the Love Dare, even destroying his home computer to remove his pornographic addictions and temptations. However, Catherine gives him an envelope with a divorce petition, leaving Caleb heartbroken.

Catherine discovers that her mother's medical equipment costs have been paid anonymously, and she erroneously believes it was Dr. Keller, bringing them closer. Caleb eventually discovers the burgeoning affair and discreetly confronts the doctor. After Caleb leaves, Dr. Keller pulls out a wedding band, revealing to the audience that he is also married, and terminates his pursuit of Catherine.

Catherine confronts Caleb after discovering his Love Dare journal, and he reveals to her that he has completed the challenge but is still following its guidelines. Despite Caleb's heartfelt apology, Catherine still needs time to reconsider the divorce. She later discovers that Caleb used his savings to pay for new medical equipment for her mother, with Dr. Keller only contributing $300. Moved by Caleb's selflessness, Catherine reconciles with him. Caleb discovers that his mother, whom he has treated poorly, did the Love Dare for his father rather than vice versa, as Caleb had initially thought. Realizing his bad behavior, he offers her an emotional apology, and she forgives him. The film ends with Caleb and Catherine renewing their wedding vows.

On the last day of my retreat, the first thing I did was grab my cell phone and ordered my copy of the Love Dare. When it arrived, I covered every identifying mark on the book's exterior with black electrical tape and secretly did the entire forty-day challenge. As I read through each daily challenge, I wrote my notes directly in the book. One of the early challenges was doing something unexpected, like picking up a gift and surprising your spouse. I thought it would be nice to do something different and get her a greeting card that let her know how I feel about her. So I headed to the store and searched the card section for the perfect card. I found three cards I liked and could not choose between them, so I got them all. The first card was a general thank-you card that told her how much I loved and appreciated her. I gave that to her the first day. The second card was bridal. I love the CSB Bible translation, so I went online, found a CSB bridal Bible, and bought it for her. When it came in, I gave it along with the card and told her how much I loved my bride. The final card was a Thanksgiving card, and I knew I would be done with the forty-day challenge around Thanksgiving. Once I completed the Love Dare, with all my handwritten notes, I removed all of the discrete markings I used to hide the book, gave her the book along with the Thanksgiving card, and told her what I had been doing in secret for her.

She had no idea what I was doing at the time, but she said she knew something was different and felt that we were drawing closer and closer every day through the process. I can sit here as I write this and tell you that it has been a life-changing experience for our marriage.

I am not saying that everyone who reads this should go out and Love Dare their spouse. What I am saying is that God made me intentional about prioritizing my relationship with my wife, and in turn, she has reciprocated that priority in her life toward me. This course correction was pivotal in building a Godly legacy for us.

So you might be asking, "What is the best way to prioritize my spouse?" Start by praying for your spouse in your quiet time and with your spouse in your time together. Make that a priority over Netflix, TikTok, Facebook, or whatever you are putting before them.

> *The family that prays together stays together.*
> —Patrick Peyton [10]

Prayer does something to us. Individual prayers are personal. When we pray *for* our spouse, we are interceding with the Lord on their behalf, but they don't know what we are praying about. When we pray *with* our spouse, we begin to hear their heart personally and are drawn closer together. Fervent, open, honest, and audible prayer with our spouse puts all our cards on display before them and God, and we become vulnerable with the person who knows us best. It creates a foundation of honesty in marriage that heals and brings us together like nothing this world offers. See where the Lord leads you in the process, and follow him together on the journey toward a healthy marriage and legacy.

---

10 "Patrick Peyton." Wikipedia, February 4, 2024. https://en.wikipedia.org/wiki/Patrick_Peyton#:~:text=Patrick%20Peyton%2C%20CSC%20(January%209,is%20a%20world%20at%20peace%22.

I want to give you something powerful to add to your toolbox: how to pray *for* and *with* your wife, and how to pray *for* and *with* your husband. I ask that you take this and make a copy to tape to the front of your Bible and use it every day in your prayer time. *Note: There will be an abridged version of this in the appendix for easier printing.*

This is something that I rely on every day to intercede for Sandra, and I made a copy of it and placed it in the front of my Bible. I did the same thing in front of her bridal Bible and asked her to do the same for me. Consider this a living and breathing guide, and add to it what the Lord puts on your heart to uplift your spouse. Prayer changes lives. If you can be disciplined in doing this, it will change your life and ensure a Godly foundation for your legacy.

How to Pray *for* and *with* Your Wife

1. Pray that she would develop a deep love for the Lord God, dedicating her heart, mind, soul, and strength to Him.

    Teacher, which command in the law is the greatest?" He said to him, "Love the Lord your God with all your heart, with all your soul, and with all your mind. This is the greatest and most important command. The second is like it: Love your neighbor as yourself. All the Law and the Prophets depend on these two commands.
    —Matthew 22:36–40

2. Pray that she discovers her beauty and identity through her relationship with Christ, reflecting His character in her life.

    In the same way, wives, submit yourselves to your own husbands so that, even if some disobey the word, they may be won over without

a word by the way their wives live when they observe your pure, reverent lives. Don't let your beauty consist of outward things like elaborate hairstyles and wearing gold jewelry or fine clothes, but rather what is inside the heart—the imperishable quality of a gentle and quiet spirit, which is of great worth in God's sight.
 —1 Peter 3:1–4

Charm is deceptive and beauty is fleeting, but a woman who fears the Lord will be praised.
 —Proverbs 31:30

3. Pray that she embraces a love for the Word of God and permits its transformative power to nurture her growth.

To make her holy, cleansing her with the washing of water by the word.
 —Ephesians 5:26

4. Pray that she will exhibit grace, communicate truth with love, and refrain from engaging in gossip.

But speaking the truth in love, let us grow in every way into him who is the head—Christ.
 —Ephesians 4:15

No foul language should come from your mouth, but only what is good for building up someone in need, so that it gives grace to those who hear.
 —Ephesians 4:29
Wives, likewise, should be worthy of respect, not slanderers, self-controlled, faithful in everything.

—1 Timothy 3:11

5. Pray that she would respect you as her husband and submit to your leadership as unto the Lord.

Wives, submit to your husbands as to the Lord, because the husband is the head of the wife as Christ is the head of the church. He is the Savior of the body. Now, as the church submits to Christ, so also wives are to submit to their husbands in everything.
—Ephesians 5:22–24

6. Pray that she would cultivate gratitude and discover her contentment in Christ rather than in her circumstances.

I rejoiced in the Lord greatly because, once again, you renewed your care for me. You were, in fact, concerned about me but lacked the opportunity to show it. I don't say this out of need, for I have learned to be content in whatever circumstances I find myself. I know how to make do with little, and I know how to make do with a lot. In any and all circumstances, I have learned the secret of being content—whether well-fed or hungry, whether in abundance or in need.
—Philippians 4:10–13

7. Pray that she would demonstrate hospitality and be diligent in serving others with the joy that reflects Christ's character.

Do nothing out of selfish ambition or conceit, but in humility

consider others as more important than yourselves. Everyone should look not to his own interests, but rather to the interests of others.
   —Philippians 2:3–4

8. Pray that she contributes goodness to her family throughout her life, avoiding any actions that may bring harm or negativity.
She rewards him with good, not evil, all the days of her life.
   —Proverbs 31:12

And his interests are divided. The unmarried woman or virgin is concerned about the things of the Lord so that she may be holy both in body and in spirit. But the married woman is concerned about the things of the world—how she may please her husband.
   —1 Corinthians 7:34

9. Pray that she seeks out and welcomes the guidance of godly older women to mentor her, aiding in her growth. Also, pray that she becomes a godly mentor to her children and younger women.

In the same way, older women are to be reverent in behavior, not slanderers, not slaves to excessive drinking. They are to teach what is good, so that they may encourage the young women to love their husbands and to love their children.
   —Titus 3:4

10. Pray that she remains steadfast in her roles as a wife and mother, not succumbing to the lies of the enemy that seek to diminish her value in those roles.

To be self-controlled, pure, workers at home, kind, and in submission to their husbands, so that God's word will not be slandered.
   —Titus 2:5

11. Pray that she embodies love, patience, resilience against offense, and a willingness to forgive quickly.

My dear brothers and sisters, understand this: Everyone should be quick to listen, slow to speak, and slow to anger.
   —James 1:19

And be kind and compassionate to one another, forgiving one another, just as God also forgave you in Christ.
   —Ephesians 4:32

12. Pray that her intimate needs are fulfilled exclusively by you, her husband, and that she can reciprocate in meeting yours.

Now in response to the matters you wrote about: "It is good for a man not to have sexual relations with a woman." But because sexual immorality is so common, each man should have sexual relations with his own wife, and each woman should have sexual relations with her own husband. A husband should fulfill his marital duty to his wife, and likewise a wife to her husband. A wife does not have the right over her own body, but her husband does. In the same way, a husband does not have the right over his own body, but his wife does. Do not deprive one another—except when you agree for a time, to devote yourselves to prayer. Then come together again; otherwise, Satan may tempt you because of your lack of self-control.
   —1 Corinthians 7:1–5

13. Pray that she remains devoted to prayer and is able to intercede effectively on behalf of others.

   Devote yourselves to prayer; stay alert in it with thanksgiving.
   —Colossians 4:2

   And was a widow for eighty-four years. She did not leave the temple, serving God night and day with fasting and prayers.
   —Luke 2:37

14. Pray that she leads her home and guides her children diligently, reflecting the character of Christ in her actions.

   She watches over the activities of her household and is never idle.
   —Proverbs 31:27

15. Pray that there be no reason for her character to be slandered or to lose confidence.
   Therefore, I want younger women to marry, have children, manage their households, and give the adversary no opportunity to accuse us.
   —1 Timothy 5:14

How to Pray *for* and *with* Your Husband

1. Pray that he develops a deep love for the Lord, dedicating his heart, mind, soul, and strength to Him.

"Teacher, which command in the law is the greatest?" He said to him, "Love the Lord your God with all your heart, with all your soul, and with all your mind. This is the greatest and most important command. The second is like it: Love your neighbor as yourself. All the Law and the Prophets depend on these two commands."
—Matthew 22:36–40

2. Pray that he walks with integrity, honoring his promises, and fulfilling his commitments.

A Description of the Godly, A psalm of David. Lord, who can dwell in your tent? Who can live on your holy mountain? The one who lives blamelessly, practices righteousness, and acknowledges the truth in his heart—who does not slander with his tongue, who does not harm his friend or discredit his neighbor, who despises the one rejected by the Lord but honors those who fear the Lord, who keeps his word whatever the cost, who does not lend his silver at interest or take a bribe against the innocent—the one who does these things will never be shaken.
—Psalm 15

The Traits of the Righteous Hallelujah! Happy is the person who fears the Lord, taking great delight in his commands. His descendants will be powerful in the land; the generation of the upright will be blessed. Wealth and riches are in his house, and his righteousness

endures forever. Light shines in the darkness for the upright. He is gracious, compassionate, and righteous. Good will come to the one who lends generously and conducts his business fairly. He will never be shaken. The righteous one will be remembered forever. He will not fear bad news; his heart is confident, trusting in the Lord. His heart is assured; he will not fear. In the end he will look in triumph on his foes. He distributes freely to the poor; his righteousness endures forever. His horn will be exalted in honor.
 —Psalms 112:1–9

3. Pray that he loves you unconditionally and remains faithful to you.

Husbands, love your wives, just as Christ loved the church and gave himself for her to make her holy, cleansing her with the washing of water by the word. He did this to present the church to himself in splendor, without spot or wrinkle or anything like that, but holy and blameless. In the same way, husbands are to love their wives as their own bodies. He who loves his wife loves himself. For no one ever hates his own flesh but provides and cares for it, just as Christ does for the church, since we are members of his body. For this reason, a man will leave his father and mother and be joined to his wife, and the two will become one flesh. This mystery is profound, but I am talking about Christ and the church. To sum up, each one of you is to love his wife as himself, and the wife is to respect her husband.
 —Ephesians 5:25–33

Now in response to the matters you wrote about: "It is good for a man not to have sexual relations with a woman." But because sexual immorality is so common, each man should have sexual relations with his own wife, and each woman should have sexual relations

with her own husband. A husband should fulfill his marital duty to his wife, and likewise a wife to her husband. A wife does not have the right over her own body, but her husband does. In the same way, a husband does not have the right over his own body, but his wife does. Do not deprive one another—except when you agree for a time, to devote yourselves to prayer. Then come together again; otherwise, Satan may tempt you because of your lack of self-control.
—1 Corinthians 7:1–5

4. Pray that he displays kindness, resilience against offense, and a willingness to forgive quickly.

My dear brothers and sisters, understand this: Everyone should be quick to listen, slow to speak, and slow to anger.
—James 1:19

And be kind and compassionate to one another, forgiving one another, just as God also forgave you in Christ.
—Ephesians 4:32

5. Pray that he remains focused and avoids passivity, embracing responsibility with determination.

Attempts to Discourage the Builders: When Sanballat, Tobiah, Geshem the Arab, and the rest of our enemies heard that I had rebuilt the wall and that no gap was left in it—though at that time I had not installed the doors in the city gates—Sanballat and Geshem sent me a message: "Come, let's meet together in the villages of the Ono Valley." They were planning to harm me. So I sent messengers to them, saying, "I am doing important work and cannot come down. Why should the work cease while I leave it and go down to you?" Four times they sent me the same proposal, and I gave them the same reply. Sanballat sent me this same message a fifth time by his aide, who had an open letter in his hand. In it was written: It is reported among the nations—and Geshem agrees—that you and the Jews plan to rebel. This is the reason you are building the wall. According to these reports, you are to become their king and have even set up the prophets in Jerusalem to proclaim on your behalf, "There is a king in Judah." These rumors will be heard by the king. So come, let's confer together. Then I replied to him, "There is nothing to these rumors you are spreading; you are inventing them in your own mind." For they were all trying to intimidate us, saying, "They will drop their hands from the work, and it will never be finished." But now, my God, strengthen my hands.

—Nehemiah 6:1–9

Attempts to Intimidate Nehemiah: I went to the house of Shemaiah son of Delaiah, son of Mehetabel, who was restricted to his house. He said: Let's meet at the house of God, inside the temple. Let's shut the temple doors because they're coming to kill you. They're coming to kill you tonight! But I said, "Should a man like me run away? How can someone like me enter the temple and live? I will not go." I realized that God had not sent him, because of the prophecy he spoke against me. Tobiah and Sanballat had hired him. He was hired, so that I would be intimidated, do as he suggested, sin, and get a bad reputation, in order that they could discredit me. My God, remember Tobiah and Sanballat for what they have done, and also the prophetess Noadiah and the other prophets who wanted to intimidate me.

—Nehemiah 6:1–14

6. Pray that he becomes a diligent worker, faithfully providing for your family and children.

Go to the ant, you slacker! Observe its ways and become wise. Without leader, administrator, or ruler, it prepares its provisions in summer; it gathers its food during harvest. How long will you stay in bed, you slacker? When will you get up from your sleep? A little sleep, a little slumber, a little folding of the arms to rest, and your poverty will come like a robber, your need, like a bandit.
—Proverbs 6:6–11

But if anyone does not provide for his own family, especially for his own household, he has denied the faith and is worse than an unbeliever.
—1 Timothy 5:8

7. Pray that he surrounds himself with wise friends and steers clear of those who may lead him astray with foolishness.

The one who walks with the wise will become wise, but a companion of fools will suffer harm.
—Proverbs 13:20

Do not be deceived: "Bad company corrupts good morals."
—1 Corinthians 15:33

8. Pray that he exercises sound judgment as he seeks justice, embraces mercy, and walks humbly with God.

Mankind, he has told each of you what is good and what it is the Lord requires of you: to act justly, to love faithfulness, and to walk humbly with your God.
  —Micah 6:8

9. Pray that he relies on God's wisdom and strength instead of his own.

Trust in the Lord with all your heart, and do not rely on your own understanding; in all your ways know him, and he will make your paths straight.
  —Proverbs 3:5

Now if any of you lacks wisdom, he should ask God—who gives to all generously and ungrudgingly—and it will be given to him.
  —James 1:5

God is working in you both to will and to work according to his good purpose.
  —Philippians 2:13

10. Pray that his decisions are rooted in reverence for God rather than fear of people.

Trust in the Lord with all your heart, and do not rely on your own understanding; in all your ways know him, and he will make your paths straight.
  —Proverbs 3:5

Now if any of you lacks wisdom, he should ask God—who gives to all generously and ungrudgingly—and it will be given to him.
   —James 1:5

For it is God who is working in you both to will and to work according to his good purpose.
   —Philippians 2:13

11. Pray that he grows into a strong spiritual leader, characterized by courage, wisdom, and unwavering conviction.

After the death of Moses the Lord's servant, the Lord spoke to Joshua son of Nun, Moses's assistant: "Moses my servant is dead. Now you and all the people prepare to cross over the Jordan to the land I am giving the Israelites. I have given you every place where the sole of your foot treads, just as I promised Moses. Your territory will be from the wilderness and Lebanon to the great river, the Euphrates River—all the land of the Hittites—and west to the Mediterranean Sea. No one will be able to stand against you as long as you live. I will be with you, just as I was with Moses. I will not leave you or abandon you. "Be strong and courageous, for you will distribute the land I swore to their ancestors to give them as an inheritance. Above all, be strong and very courageous to observe carefully the whole instruction my servant Moses commanded you. Do not turn from it to the right or the left, so that you will have success wherever you go. This book of instruction must not depart from your mouth; you are to meditate on it day and night so that you may carefully observe everything written in it. For then you will prosper and succeed in whatever you do. Haven't I commanded you: be strong and courageous? Do not be afraid or discouraged, for the Lord your

God is with you wherever you go." Then Joshua commanded the officers of the people."
—Joshua 1:1–10

But if it doesn't please you to worship the Lord, choose for yourselves today: Which will you worship—the gods your ancestors worshiped beyond the Euphrates River or the gods of the Amorites in whose land you are living? As for me and my family, we will worship the Lord."
—Joshua 24:15

12. Pray that he is liberated from any bondage, negative habits, or addictions that hinder his progress.

Then Jesus said to the Jews who had believed him, "If you continue in my word, you really are my disciples."
—John 8:31

So if the Son sets you free, you really will be free.
—John 8:36

What should we say then? Should we continue in sin so that grace may multiply? Absolutely not! How can we who died to sin still live in it? Or are you unaware that all of us who were baptized into Christ Jesus were baptized into his death? Therefore, we were buried with him by baptism into death, in order that, just as Christ was raised from the dead by the glory of the Father, so we too may walk in newness of life. For if we have been united with him in the likeness of his death, we will certainly also be in the likeness of his resurrection. For we know that our old self was crucified with him so that the body ruled by sin might be rendered powerless so that we may no longer be enslaved to sin, since a person who has died is freed from sin. Now if we died with Christ, we believe that

we will also live with him, because we know that Christ, having been raised from the dead, will not die again. Death no longer rules over him. For the death he died, he died to sin once for all time; but the life he lives, he lives to God. So, you too consider yourselves dead to sin and alive to God in Christ Jesus. Therefore do not let sin reign in your mortal body, so that you obey its desires. And do not offer any parts of it to sin as weapons for unrighteousness. But as those who are alive from the dead, offer yourselves to God, and all the parts of yourselves to God as weapons for righteousness. For sin will not rule over you, because you are not under the law but under grace. What then? Should we sin because we are not under the law but under grace? Absolutely not! Don't you know that if you offer yourselves to someone as obedient slaves, you are slaves of that one you obey—either of sin leading to death or of obedience leading to righteousness? But thank God that, although you used to be slaves of sin, you obeyed from the heart that pattern of teaching to which you were handed over, and having been set free from sin, you became enslaved to righteousness. I am using a human analogy because of the weakness of your flesh. For just as you offered the parts of yourselves as slaves to impurity, and to greater and greater lawlessness, so now offer them as slaves to righteousness, which results in sanctification.
 —Romans 6:1–19

13. Pray that he discovers his identity and fulfillment in God rather than in temporary pleasures or possessions.

Take delight in the Lord, and he will give you your heart's desires.
 —Psalms 37:4

Do not love the world or the things in the world. If anyone loves the world, the love of the Father is not in him. For everything in the world—the lust of the flesh, the lust of the eyes, and the pride in one's possessions—is not from the Father, but is from the world. And the world with its lust is passing away, but the one who does the will of God remains forever.
 —1 John 2:15–17

14. Pray that he regularly reads and allows the Word of God to direct his choices and actions.

Your word is a lamp for my feet and a light on my path.
 —Psalms 119:105

"Therefore, everyone who hears these words of mine and acts on them will be like a wise man who built his house on the rock. The rain fell, the rivers rose, and the winds blew and pounded that house. Yet it didn't collapse, because its foundation was on the rock. But everyone who hears these words of mine and doesn't act on them will be like a foolish man who built his house on the sand. The rain fell, the rivers rose, the winds blew and pounded that house, and it collapsed. It collapsed with a great crash."
 —Matthew 7:24–27

15. Pray that he remains faithful to God and leaves behind a powerful legacy for future generations to follow.

For I am already being poured out as a drink offering, and the time for my departure is close. I have fought the good fight, I have finished the race, I have kept the faith. There is reserved for me the

crown of righteousness, which the Lord, the righteous Judge, will give me on that day, and not only to me, but to all those who have loved his appearing.
—2 Timothy 4:6–8

I have glorified you on the earth by completing the work you gave me to do.
—John 17:4

Priority 2: Your Spouse—Reflection and Application

1. Take some time to think about your marriage covenant. Ask the Lord for guidance on how to fulfill your duties properly.
2. In what way would your marriage benefit from daily prayer with your spouse?
3. What are my spouse's needs and fears, and how can I help meet them?
4. How can we embrace suffering together as a couple?
5. How can we keep the romance alive in our marriage?
6. How can I take the initiative to resolve conflict?
7. Do my words edify my spouse?

PRIORITY 3: YOUR FAMILY

If you were to put this book down right now, open an internet browser of your choice, and search "broken home statistics and the effect on society," you would quickly become discouraged by the divorce statistics in the United States and other parts of the world. While that statistic itself is devastating enough, if you were to continue to scroll down the result page and read just the highlights, it starts to become very clear that the effect of broken homes causes not only a significant strain on social welfare systems and public resources but also that broken families contribute to social fragmentation and disintegration of society. If you were to start opening the highlighted results and reading the content, you would quickly realize how many people have intentionally failed to build a Godly legacy.

Strong families are the bedrock of social cohesion, fostering a sense of belonging, trust, and mutual support within communities.

What does a strong family look like? Maybe you never had one, or perhaps you came from a messed-up family, or maybe you messed up your own family. Know that every family has the potential to be a Godly family and that it is never too late to make a course correction and get back on track. Just put your priorities back in order.

A Godly family pleases God, knows, fears, and serves God, and trains its children and generations in the ways of the Lord.

The characteristics of a Godly family include, but are not limited to:

1. A Godly family serves the Lord together.
2. A Godly family seeks God.
3. A Godly family speaks truth.
4. A Godly family shows unconditional love.
5. A Godly family stays humble.
6. A Godly family is united.
7. A Godly family forgives.

Nothing is more critical to the stability of the family than witnessing a father and mother who demonstrate love and respect for Christ and each other in front of their children.

Fathers, if you want your son to treat his mother well, you must treat her well in front of him. If you want your daughters to marry Godly men, show them what they should look for in a man in the way you treat their mother. Raise their expectations of what a king looks like, and your princesses set high standards.

One of my favorite "man movies" is *Fight Club*, starring Brad Pitt and Edward Norton. If you haven't seen it, I don't recommend it. It is not exactly a wholesome movie. I won't go into the details of what this movie is about. But I bring it up because a notable quote from the film illustrates this point so well: "Our fathers were our role models for God. If our fathers bailed, what does that tell you about God? Listen to me! You have to consider the possibility that God does not like you." [11]

I know this is a fictitious Hollywood quote, but it is profound.

Biblical passages such as Isaiah 7:15–16 indicate that there is such a thing as an "age of accountability." Unfortunately, Scripture gives us no

---

[11] "Fight Club." IMDb. Accessed April 1, 2024. https://www.imdb.com/title/tt0137523/characters/nm0000093.

guidelines for determining when a child crosses that decisive threshold into adult life.

> *By the time he learns to reject what is bad and choose what is good, he will be eating butter and honey.*
> —Isaiah 7:15

> *For before the boy knows to reject what is bad and choose what is good, the land of the two kings you dread will be abandoned.*
> —Isaiah 7:16

Fathers, don't think for one second that your children are not watching you and wanting to be just like you. If we are not setting a Godly example for them to follow before they reach the age of reason and accountability, they will be susceptible to the lies of the enemy. Lies like the one from Fight Club: "Listen to me! You have to consider the possibility that God does not like you."

We will fail from time to time as fathers. The Heavenly Father is the only perfect Father. What matters is that when we fail, we must look to the perfect Father for direction and demonstrate our resolve before our children. They have to know that it is OK to fail so that they can see that they can recover.

BIBLICAL LEGACY AND FAMILY LINEAGE

Lineage is an important concept in the Bible and has direct ties to legacy. For the Hebrew people, genealogies were a normal way of life because they passed their history down orally; written documentation was not a thing back then. Family stories were told to children, who passed them on to their children, and so on. This helped them not only remember each of their ancestors but also the promises from God.

Matthew begins with a genealogy that shows the line from Adam to Jesus. Luke also has a genealogy, and there are three sets of genealogical lists in Genesis. Two are in chapter 4, referring to Cain and Seth, and chapter 5 expands on Seth's line. There is also another list in 1 Chronicles.

Typically, a particular family genealogy is only of interest to the family it references. The Bible is our genealogy because everyone on earth can claim Adam and Eve as their ancestors, as they were created in the beginning, and it contains written stories of all of those who came before us. We are all a part of the legacy of Adam and Eve.

The genealogy listed in the Bible is not exhaustive by any means and was purposed to show the lineage of Adam to David to Jesus. Every instance in the Bible that speaks to genealogy is male (paternal). For example, Cain was the son of Adam, Solomon was the son of David, who was some of Jesse, etcetera. However, the mother was also important because it was the bloodline of the mother that determined whether you were Jewish or not.

This was an essential concept for the Hebrew people. Native-born membership of the Jewish people comes through the mother, but tribal affiliation comes through the father. This system existed to ensure that Jews would not marry non-Jews. If a Jewish man married a non-Jewish woman, the kids would not be considered Jewish and could not inherit his name or tribe. A Jewish woman who married a non-Jewish husband would have Jewish kids with no tribal status and would be born with the status of "fatherless orphans." In the tribal society of that day, being without a tribe meant that you were without social support and would probably end up in a lower social class. In ancient Israelite society, orphans (in Hebrew mamzerim), meaning children of illegitimate unions, along with converts to Judaism and other Jews unable to claim the protection of a tribe or family, were usually charity cases that needed to be supported by the community.

So the message is the same today as it was yesterday. The father and the mother play a significant role in their family's lives. We are all downline blood recipients of someone else's legacy, and our place, to the point of the "age of accountability," is based on the characteristics and actions of those who preceded us. Good or bad, we had no control to that point. What we do from there is up to us.

Just like in the biblical stories, we learn just as much of *what to do* as we do *what not to do* from our fathers and mothers. There is no definitive parental guide that anyone has ever written that tells us how to do this; we must rely on the Holy Spirit.

Are we destined to become like our parents? The trends say yes, and contrary to popular culture, this is a good thing. It doesn't matter whether your parents were good parents or bad parents; what matters is that we know and recognize that we will likely be similar to them at some point. We have witnessed the good and the bad firsthand and can make a conscious effort to replicate the good and break the cycle of bad things for all future generations of our bloodline.

Once we reach the "age of accountability" and adulthood, we can no longer blame our parents for our faults. We have to take responsibility for our own lives and end generational curses.

> *The person who sins is the one who will die. A son won't suffer punishment for the father's iniquity, and a father won't suffer punishment for the son's iniquity.*
> —Ezekiel 18:20

OVERCOMING GENERATIONAL CURSES

A generational curse is a habit or behavior passed from generation to generation. Parents should strive to make sure that the life they lead will help their children live a better one. Children practice what they have learned and gathered from generations before them. This is not automatically a terrible thing; however, how does this align with where you are in your own life? The lessons you were taught when you were younger can be a guide for you later in life. If you want to see the trajectory of where your family will end up, looking back often paints a clear picture.

A generational curse is going to be different for each of us. Maybe your father had anger issues, and you recognize that and make a conscious effort to be patient and understanding. Maybe your mother drank too much and was unhealthy and shrewd, and you make a conscious effort to break that cycle. Maybe your parents were barely able to make ends meet and never saved any money, and you chose to better yourself by going to school and getting an education that enabled you to get a better job and save for your future. Or your parents were just not there for you, and you choose to always be there for your children.

It is never too late to make a positive change that breaks the generational curses for future generations.

> *If my people, which are called by my name, shall humble themselves, and pray, and seek my face, and turn from their wicked ways; then will I hear from heaven, and will forgive their sin, and will heal their land.*
> —2 Chronicles 7:14

Priority 3: Your Family—Reflection and Application

1. Decide whom you will serve: God or man. Sit down with your spouse (if you are married) and discuss what is seen, heard, and done in your house. Does it please the Lord?
2. How can I cultivate a legacy of gratitude? You may want to have a blank journal and ask family members to write one or more blessings daily.
3. Encourage your children to pray with you when making tough decisions, interceding for others, or asking for material provisions. As they see God answer prayers, they will learn to look to him when they are in need.
4. Create an atmosphere of understanding. Welcome your children's questions about faith and family. What does that look like in your household?
5. Am I an example of the character traits I would like to develop in my children?
6. Am I intentionally pursuing a relationship with each of my children?
7. Am I being a good shepherd to my family?
8. Call your children to a spiritual mission of what God wants to do in their lives.

PRIORITY 4: YOUR WORK

I am sure some of you may be wondering why a book on leaving a Godly legacy would have you prioritize your work over your ministry, and that is a great question. The reason is that our family is our first ministry, and we must provide for them. If you are fortunate enough that ministry is your means of providing for your family, then you are extra blessed. I do not fall into this category.

I want to take a moment to refocus on what this book is about. It is about being purposeful in building a Godly legacy. Legacy is something that is passed on, and it can take many forms. It is totally up to you as to what you are going to leave behind. A legacy may be of one's faith, ethics, and core values, or it may be monetary or comprised of assets. A Godly legacy is being purposeful in prioritizing the priorities in life in accordance with the Word of God.

Why is it important to redefine this again at this stage? The reason is that the worldly view of legacy differs from the Godly view of legacy. Living worldly means living as the world does. Its standard is based on people's experiences, opinions, and thoughts. Living Godly means living Godlike, based on the standards of what God says.

This is important to understand as we explore the concept of prioritizing work in relationship to building our legacy. Perhaps it is best summarized in these two passages of scripture: "For the love of money is a root of all kinds of evil, and by craving it, some have wandered away from the faith and pierced themselves with many pains" (1 Tim.

6:10) and "Set your minds on what is above, not on what is on the earth" (Col. 3:2).

Let's address the obvious elephant in the room. Why do we have to work? Why can we not just rely on God to provide everything for us?

Let's take a minute to discover what the Bible says about work.

As beings created in God's image, we share his communicable attributes; that is, we are like him in certain ways. For example, God is productive—he creates, builds, maintains, repairs, and protects his handiwork. God is busy. He is not idle; as living souls made in his image, we should not be idle creatures.

> *Then God said, "Let us make man in our image, according to our likeness. They will rule the fish of the sea, the birds of the sky, the livestock, the whole earth, and the creatures that crawl on the earth."*
> —Genesis 1:26

Looking at the Garden of Eden before the fall, you can see that it fits the description of paradise in every way, yet the first couple, Adam and Eve, did not spend their days and nights lazing about in hammocks sipping on Mai Tais in paradise. God gave them dominion over creation, and with that dominion came responsibility. Adam and Eve kept busy. And so should we. The picture becomes even more evident as we dig in further: we are meant to work.

> *The Lord God took the man and placed him in the garden of Eden to work it and watch over it.*
> —Genesis 2:15

King Solomon addresses the concept of work and the consequences of laziness throughout the book of Proverbs. In Proverbs 6:6–11, Solomon offers a rebuke to the lazy.

Go to the ant, you slacker! Observe its ways and become wise. Without leader, administrator, or ruler, it prepares its provisions in summer; it gathers its food during harvest. How long will you stay in bed, you slacker? When will you get up from your sleep? A little sleep, a little slumber, a little folding of the arms to rest, and your poverty will come like a robber, your need, like a bandit.

Diligence represents the careful and persistent effort or work required to provide. The goal is not solely to amass material wealth but rather to avoid becoming a burden to others or bringing disgrace to your family or church. Ants serve as a diligent example compared to lazy individuals. There is wisdom to be gained from even the smallest insects, and their industrious nature can put us to shame. Unfortunately, habits of laziness and excess tend to take hold and gradually lead to a wasteful and impoverished life.

This passage explains that our work must first provide for the necessities of our household before we splurge on conveniences: "Complete your outdoor work and prepare your field; afterward, build your house" (Prov. 24:27).

We see from the very beginning of the Bible that God created. We see he is the ultimate worker and made man to work the fields and care for his creation.

The apostle Paul further chastised those who will not support their families as being worse than infidels: "But if anyone does not provide for his own, that is his own household, he has denied the faith and is worse than an unbeliever" (1 Tim. 5:8).

In addition, Paul, whose tireless missionary efforts spanned the far reaches of the known world, heartily condemns idleness:

Now we command you, brothers, in the name of our Lord Jesus Christ, to keep away from every brother who walks irresponsibly and not according to the tradition received from us. For you yourselves know how you must imitate us: We were not irresponsible among you; we did not eat anyone's food free of charge; instead, we labored and struggled, working night and day, so that we would not be a burden to any of you. It is not that we don't have the right to support, but we did it to make ourselves an example to you so that you would imitate us. In fact, when we were with you, this is what we commanded you: "If anyone isn't willing to work, he should not eat." For we hear that there are some among you who walk irresponsibly, not working at all, but interfering with the work of others. Now we command and exhort such people by the Lord Jesus Christ that quietly working, they may eat their own food. Brothers, do not grow weary in doing good. (2 Thess. 3:6–12)

We were created to work, but with this said, we were not made as machines without an off switch. Extreme exhaustion and burnout are not Godly virtues: "On the seventh day God had completed his work that he had done, and he rested on the seventh day from all his work that he had done" (Gen. 2:2).

Just as God "rested" on the seventh day of creation, we must regularly set aside our labors for rest, reflection, and recreation. A day of rest is for our benefit. God wants us to place our tools back in the box, tend to our families, ease our minds and bodies, and devote time to him. We are to be still and know that he is God: "Be still, and know that I am God, exalted among the nations, exalted on the earth" (Ps. 46:10).

PURSUIT OF WHAT MATTERS

We spent countless hours learning a trade and often continue to pursue professional development opportunities to advance our careers in pursuit of money, or power. If we are not careful, the drive to succeed in business and life will surpass our desire for everything else, and we start to look at our job as our identity. I can recall countless instances where, in meeting someone new, as we were shaking hands, they would say, "Hello, I'm John Doe, and I am the director of marketing at company XYZ." This makes a lot of sense in a business meeting, but when you are sitting in a small group or men's ministry, it sounds a little bit out of place, and I often wonder if this new acquaintance is a workaholic who neglects his family.

As a provider, there is a time and a place to focus on career growth. I do not deny this. I have several degrees, including a master's degree, and I try to dedicate at least an hour a day to professional development. This is a good pursuit, but not if it comes at a cost to your other priorities in life.

TRUSTING IN GOD TO PROVIDE

As I started to seek inspiration from the Lord in writing this section, I realized there was a general misunderstanding of the concept of "trusting in God to provide." Therefore, I feel it is necessary to add this section to the Work Priority chapter.

This started with a discussion I was having with my nephew, who was about to join the US Air Force. He was helping me build a fireplace in the living room. As we were working, we began to talk about life and the air force, and I asked him if he was going to put money into his GI Bill.

If you are unfamiliar with the GI Bill, I will explain. When you enter the air force, you can sign up for the Montgomery GI Bill, and they will take out $100 a month for the first year of service. Then, it pays for thirty-six months of education benefits that can be used for college or technical schools. It is a great benefit, and I was able to pay for my master's degree with my GI Bill benefits years after my service was done.

I asked him if he was planning on contributing to it. He said he'd never had any real money before and was planning on staying in the air force, but he was unsure if he would want to attend college. I encouraged him to contribute to the system and that he had time to figure out how to use it later. I also told him there are options to transfer it to his kids later if he decides not to use it. He was encouraged to hear that and said yes, uncle, I think that is wise. I told him that when my initial twelve months of payments were done, I took that money and sent it to a savings account that I later rolled into a 401(k) to begin saving for my future retirement.

He looked at me oddly and said, "Don't you trust God will provide for you?" This implied that I was taking it out of God's hands. I was a little perplexed by his comment. I thought to myself, *What? Who taught him that?* I paused for a bit before replying. It was a good question, and I felt it was a perfect time to do some teaching. I asked him if he had ever heard the parable of the talents and proceeded to tell him the story from Matthew 25:14–30:

> For it is just like a man about to go on a journey. He called his own servants and entrusted his possessions to them. To one he gave five talents, to another two talents, and to another one talent, depending on each one's ability. Then he went on a journey. Immediately the man who had received five talents went, put them to work, and earned five more. In the same way the man with two earned two more. But the man who had received one talent went off, dug a hole in the ground, and hid his master's money. After a long time, the master of those servants came and settled accounts with them. The man who had received five talents approached, presented five more talents, and said, 'Master, you gave me five talents. See, I've earned five more talents.' "His master said to him, 'Well done, good and

faithful servant! You were faithful over a few things; I will put you in charge of many things. Share your master's joy.' "The man with two talents also approached. He said, 'Master, you gave me two talents. See, I've earned two more talents.' His master said to him, 'Well done, good and faithful servant! You were faithful over a few things; I will put you in charge of many things. Share your master's joy.' "The man who had received one talent also approached and said, 'Master, I know you. You're a harsh man, reaping where you haven't sown and gathering where you haven't scattered seed. So I was afraid and went off and hid your talent in the ground. See, you have what is yours.' "His master replied to him, 'You evil, lazy servant! If you knew that I reap where I haven't sown and gather where I haven't scattered, then you should have deposited my money with the bankers, and I would have received my money back with interest when I returned. "'So, take the talent from him and give it to the one who has ten talents. For to everyone who has, more will be given, and he will have more than enough. But from the one who does not have, even what he has will be taken away from him. And throw this good-for-nothing servant into the outer darkness, where there will be weeping and gnashing of teeth.'" (Matt. 25:14–30)

When I finished, I told him that trusting in God does not mean taking his blessings and doing nothing with them. Rather, we are to take them, use them, and pass them along to multiply them for his glory.

We are called to be good stewards of our money and resources. Saving for your future does not mean we are not relying on God to provide. It means that we have received an abundance from him and are being good stewards of what we have received. In the case of setting aside money for retirement, it means that we put money away while we have the ability so that we are not a burden on our family or society when we can no longer perform the work.

We were created to work. It is the means through which we support our family. Work is a blessing; it is one of the ways God provides for us. It doesn't always feel like a blessing, especially when work is stressful, but our labor provides for the necessities of life. If we are good stewards with our money, do not overindulge in the pleasures of this world, and do not take on excessive debt, we can bless others, live a full life, and leave a fantastic legacy.

Do not feel ashamed if you cannot leave wealth behind or have not amassed assets to pass down to your children. You are not a failure. If you know you cannot leave a monetary asset behind, then choose the gift of time and memories to leave behind. If you are blessed to do both, take time to get on your knees and thank the Lord God for the many blessings.

Father, I confess I sometimes forget that you are my ultimate provider. May my gratitude for your provision lead to making your great deeds known to those around me so that they may trust you. All glory and honor to you. Amen.

Priority 4: Your Work—Reflection and Application

1. Take a moment to reflect on the following statement: work makes you live, and family will feed your life. Ask yourself what you are prioritizing.
2. Work is important, but it should never be at the expense of your family. Rather than feeling guilty for dedicating time to work, how can you spend that energy on being fully present when you are with your family?

PRIORITY 5: YOUR MINISTRY

Ministry is the devoted service offered to the Lord, and any theological exploration of ministry would be lacking without focusing on the term itself. The study of the origin of words, known as etymology, sheds light on the fascinating history of the term "ministry." In the Greek language of the New Testament, this term consistently revolves around engaging in acts of service toward others. At times, it carries a profound connotation of servitude or being a devoted servant to God. Consequently, ministry conveys a sense of being obligated to work under God's authority as a loyal servant.

HOW CAN WE BE THE MOST EFFECTIVE IN MINISTRY?

Ministry is most effective when we understand whose authority we operate in and how powerful the authority is.

Between 346 and 336 BC, when major Greek city-states were already under submission, Phillip II of Macedonia directed a warning to Sparta.[12] He declared, "If I invade Laconia, I shall turn you out," indicating his

---

[12] "Philip II of Macedon." Wikipedia, February 22, 2024. https://en.wikipedia.org/wiki/Philip_II_of_Macedon#:~:text=With%20key%20Greek%20city%2Dstates,the%20Spartans%20from%20various%20parts.

intention to expel them if they did not comply. This served as a clear threat, suggesting that he would burn their fields and demolish their cities if they refused. In response, the Spartans defiantly replied with just one word: "if."

Sparta, situated in Laconia in ancient Greece, stood out as a prominent city-state. Distinguished by its distinctive social system and constitution, Sparta was a society that prioritized military excellence above all else, directing all social institutions toward rigorous military training and physical development. Spartan men, from birth, underwent a demanding training regimen, contributing to the reputation of the Spartan phalanx brigades as being widely acknowledged as the best in battle.

Why were they so confident? They were confident because of their immense preparation and willingness to give their lives for the greater good of their society because they believed in their system. It is why there are so many inspirational and legendary tales about them.

Every element of our time spent seeking the Lord is preparation to overcome the enemy who threatens to steal, kill, and destroy. The more time we spend in the word and in prayer and intercession, the stronger we are to stand against the enemy and to proclaim the authority given to us in the name of Jesus so that when the enemy comes and tells us to give up, or he will burn our fields and tear down our cities that we have built up figuratively in the form of our legacy. We can declare in the name of Jesus with complete confidence and respond accordingly: "if" or "if only."

"If" was a call of defiance by the Spartans. It was an "I dare you to try" statement. The word tells us what we are to be fearful of and then tells us not to fear anything else because God is with us.

> *Above all, fear the LORD and worship him faithfully with all your heart; consider the great things he has done for you.*
> —1 Samuel 12:24

Do not fear, for I am with you; do not be afraid, for I am your God. I will strengthen you, help you; I will hold on to you with my righteous right hand.
—Isaiah 41:10

PREPARATION FOR MINISTRY

You do not need to attend seminary school to operate in ministry. It helps, and I am not diminishing the importance, but it is not required. Most of the disciples were not trained for the work of ministry when they were called; whether you know it or not, there is a calling on your life.

This is evident when you consider legacy. Remember, you will leave a legacy of some kind no matter what. That is the calling. Being intentional about building a legacy is working within the calling.

The most personally satisfying ministry is done when we operate within our calling. The reason is that once we know our calling, we are more passionate about operating in it. Every one of us is fearfully and wonderfully made. We are unique creations with unique characteristics and traits, each called to operate differently for a specific purpose. However, there will be times when ministry presents itself, and you know deep down inside that you are not operating within what you perceive to be your calling and are out of your comfort zone. The Lord equips those he sends, and while it may not be as personally satisfying at the time to operate in this capacity, the equipping the Lord does through our preparation and quiet time is very effective if we are careful to seek guidance from the Holy Spirit.

Preach the word; be ready in season and out of season; correct, rebuke, and encourage with great patience and teaching.
—2 Timothy 4:2

We must remain ready at all times. You never know when a ministry opportunity will arise.

MAKING THE MOST OF YOUR CALLING

How can you find the time in the business of life to prepare and focus? It takes a commitment and purpose. There is plenty of time if you're willing to make the sacrifice.

Early morning is a special time of day, and many books, like *The 5AM Club*, discuss this. The principles of *The 5AM Club* state that "the first hours of the day are where heroes are made. If you want to master your life, start by owning the mornings. Freedom from distraction at 5:00 a.m. will allow you to build your creativity, maximize your fitness, and protect your serenity in an age of complexity." [13]

This concept is so profound that we should apply it to our daily lives. If you want to be most effective in ministry and building your legacy, take advantage of distraction-free times to hear the still, small voice, as the prophet Elijah did.

ELIJAH'S ENCOUNTER WITH THE LORD

> *Suddenly, the word of the Lord came to him, and he said to him, "What are you doing here, Elijah?" He replied, "I have been very zealous for the Lord God of Armies, but the Israelites have abandoned your covenant, torn down your altars, and killed your prophets with the sword. I alone am left, and they are looking for me to take my life." Then he said, "Go out and stand on the mountain in the Lord's*

---

13 Sharma, Robin S. The 5 am club: Own your morning, elevate your life. Mumbai, India: Jaico Publishing House, 2019.

presence." At that moment, the Lord passed by. A great and mighty wind was tearing at the mountains and was shattering cliffs before the Lord, but the Lord was not in the wind. After the wind there was an earthquake, but the Lord was not in the earthquake. After the earthquake there was a fire, but the Lord was not in the fire. And after the fire there was a voice, a soft whisper. When Elijah heard it, he wrapped his face in his mantle and went out and stood at the entrance of the cave. Suddenly, a voice came to him and said, "What are you doing here, Elijah?" "I have been very zealous for the Lord God of Armies," he replied, "but the Israelites have abandoned your covenant, torn down your altars, and killed your prophets with the sword. I alone am left, and they're looking for me to take my life." Then the Lord said to him, "Go and return by the way you came to the Wilderness of Damascus. When you arrive, you are to anoint Hazael as king over Aram. You are to anoint Jehu son of Nimshi as king over Israel and Elisha son of Shaphat from Abel-meholah as prophet in your place. Then Jehu will put to death whoever escapes the sword of Hazael, and Elisha will put to death whoever escapes the sword of Jehu. But I will leave seven thousand in Israel—every knee that has not bowed to Baal and every mouth that has not kissed him."

—1 Kings 19:9–18

In this passage, we can draw a parallel between the wind, the earthquake, and the fire with the distractions of social media, electronic devices, television, and work. The word teaches that God spoke to him in the quiet in a small voice, and if our life is consumed with distractions, we will miss his voice. As Elijah had to come to a quiet place to hear his voice, so do we, and it is best to do that when we are most receptive to hearing it, before the activities of the day take control of our thoughts.

Let me give you an example of how I apply this principle in my life. The Lord stirred up a yearning and desire in my heart to seek him like never before during my Quest retreat. I made a conscious and deliberate effort to make some changes in my life. I started setting my alarm clock to go off at 5:30 a.m. every morning, even before I had ever heard of the book *The 5AM Club*, and committed to reading his Word, seeking understanding through prayer, and meditating with him daily.

My typical routine is to wake when the alarm goes off, thank him for waking me, and before I get out of bed, I declare that this is the day that the Lord has made and tell him that I will rejoice and be glad in it. I then exercise for twenty to twenty-five minutes, just long enough to break a sweat, shower, and start interceding for the day. I have found that my mind is not distracted by anything at this early hour. When I am done, I finish getting ready as quietly as possible so that I do not disturb the rest of the house, and by 6:00 a.m., I am usually in the kitchen starting the coffee pot and letting the dogs out. I grab my coffee, and if it is not too cold, I sit out on the back patio by the gas fire pit and take my Bible, journal, and a highlighter out of my backpack. Before I begin, I take the Bible in my hand, place it near my heart or mouth, and ask the Lord to speak to me through his Word, asking him to reveal his purpose to me and thank him beforehand because I know he will do it.

This routine has awoken my spirit and refreshed every aspect of my life. I wake up earlier every day with a desire to spend time with the Lord like never before. When you truly experience the presence of the Lord, your heart grows fond, and you seek it more and more in every moment. Your mindset shifts to look at everything differently. God elevates your sight and lets you see things from a new perspective.

Priority 5: Your Ministry—Reflection and Application

The C. S. Lewis Institute created a list of ten questions to ask yourself to ensure you are still growing, which I have referred to ever since I first read it.

Questions to ask yourself to see if you are still growing in the Lord: Are you more like Jesus than you were a year ago?[14]

1. Are you thirstier for God than ever before?
2. Are you more and more loving?
3. Are you more sensitive to and aware of God than ever before?
4. Are you governed more and more by God's Word?
5. Are you concerned more and more with the physical and spiritual needs of others?
6. Are you increasingly concerned with the church and the kingdom of God?
7. Are the disciples of the Christian life more and more important to you?
8. Are you more and more aware of your sin?
9. you more and more willing to forgive others?

---

[14] "10 Questions to Ask to Make Sure You're Still Growing." C.S. Lewis Institute, December 22, 2023. https://www.cslewisinstitute.org/resources/10-questions-to-ask-to-make-sure-youre-still-growing/.

APPLICATION

Go ahead, admit it. If you've gotten this far and are still with me, then something has risen up inside you, and you are starting to see the picture of your legacy in your mind.

It's time for meat and potatoes, or better yet, it's time to make a meat-and-potatoes type of decision. You know the kind of decision I'm talking about. It starts with a feeling, like hunger. You think, "Hey, I'm hungry," and then ask yourself, "What am I in the mood for? How can I satisfy this hunger?" Then it comes to you: "I think a steak sounds good, but where can I get the best steak?" Then you realize that you don't have the money for the best steakhouse in town and go through all the options and end up at a decent steakhouse of your choice. The waitress brings you the menu, and you look through the options. Do you go with the New York strip, the filet mignon, the ribeye, or the T-bone? Then, on to the side dishes. What's the best way to prepare the potatoes? Baked, french fried, or au gratin?

I just realized I shouldn't have written all this just before lunch because I am now hungry.

The choices can be overwhelming, but if we don't make a decision, then the feeling of being hungry will not be satisfied. Note: if you're a vegetarian or a vegan, don't make this weird. Just think of your favorite whatever you eat, and go with it. Much love to you, though. It worked for Daniel, Shadrach, Meshach, and Abednego.

That feeling you get when you think about your family and the picture that God gives you to care for and love them drives the desire to be purposeful in building a lasting and Godly legacy. Just like picking the proper meal to satisfy your hunger, there are many intentional decisions that you must make along the path of life to better your legacy. This will look different for everyone, but there are a few essential things to ask yourself to apply the lessons learned in this book to your legacy.

Let's figure out a plan for being purposeful in building your legacy. A legacy takes a lifetime to build, so do not expect to have everything figured out right out of the gate. We walk one step at a time and eventually get somewhere. Small changes may not seem like much at the time, but over time, these many small changes that we make add up to big changes.

REFLECTION

Be honest and journal your thoughts; take what you wrote to the Lord in prayer and ask him for guidance.

1. Take a few moments to close your eyes and imagine sitting at your own memorial service.
    a. What does it look like?
    b. Who is there?
    c. What would you say about yourself if you were standing on that podium?
2. Who are the people in your life that you care the most about?
    a. Why are they important to you?
    b. If you could give them anything, what would it be?
3. Take a few minutes to reflect on the things that take your time, energy, and focus. Ask yourself if my priorities are in proper alignment.

4. Read the statement of purpose below and commit. Or write your own. This is your legacy. Commit the rest of your life to making it a reality.

STATEMENT OF PURPOSE

As a man or woman of faith, I am deeply committed to leaving a lasting Godly legacy for my family. I believe that true wealth lies not in material possessions but in the richness of one's character and the depth of one's relationship with God. Therefore, my purpose is to build a foundation of faith, love, and integrity that will serve as an enduring inheritance for generations to come.

ACTIONS TO TAKE

1. Strengthening spiritual foundations. I will prioritize nurturing a deep and authentic relationship with God within my family. This will involve regular prayer, studying Scripture together, and participating in acts of worship as a family unit. By demonstrating the importance of faith in our lives, I aim to instill in my family members a firm foundation upon which they can build their own spiritual journeys.
2. Modeling Godly character. I recognize the importance of leading by example. In all aspects of my life, I will strive to embody the virtues of love, compassion, honesty, and humility. By consistently demonstrating Godly character traits, I hope to inspire my family members to emulate these qualities in their own lives, thus perpetuating a legacy of integrity and righteousness.
3. Prioritizing family relationships. Family is a precious gift from God, and I am committed to cherishing and nurturing these relationships. I will make it a priority to spend quality time with

each family member, fostering deep bonds of love, trust, and respect. By creating a supportive and nurturing family environment, I aim to cultivate strong interpersonal connections that will endure through the generations.

4. Teaching life lessons and values. I will take every opportunity to impart valuable life lessons and Godly values to my family members. Through meaningful conversations, storytelling, and shared experiences, I will teach them the importance of kindness, forgiveness, perseverance, and gratitude. These timeless principles will serve as guiding lights, helping my family navigate life's challenges with wisdom and grace.
5. Investing in education and personal growth. I believe in the power of knowledge and continuous personal growth. Therefore, I will encourage my family members to pursue education, both formal and informal, that enriches their minds and spirits. I will provide support, guidance, and resources to help them fulfill their potential and pursue their passions, equipping them to make meaningful contributions to the world around them.
6. Creating a legacy of service. Finally, I am committed to instilling in my family members a heart for service and compassion. Together, we will seek out opportunities to serve others, both within our community and beyond. By modeling selflessness and generosity, I hope to inspire my family to make a positive impact in the world, leaving a legacy of love and compassion that reflects the heart of God.

In all that I do, my ultimate goal is to honor God and leave behind a legacy that glorifies him. May his grace and wisdom guide me in this noble endeavor, and may the legacy of faith, love, and integrity that I leave for my family be a testament to His goodness and faithfulness through the generations to come.

I, _____, hereby affirm my commitment to the statement of purpose outlined above, intended to serve as a lasting Godly legacy for my family. I acknowledge that the actions described herein reflect my sincere beliefs and intentions, and I pledge to uphold the principles outlined in this document to the best of my ability.

Furthermore, I understand that this statement of purpose is a personal declaration of my values and aspirations and does not constitute a legally binding contract. It is my intention that this document serves as a guiding framework for my conduct and decision-making, both now and in the future.

Signed: _____

Date:_____

CONCLUSION

As we come to the end of this book on building a Godly legacy, let us reflect on the journey we have undertaken together. Throughout these pages, we have explored the timeless principles and practices that form the foundation of a lasting legacy rooted in faith, love, and integrity.

We have learned that true wealth is not measured in material possessions, but in the richness of our relationships and the depth of our character. By prioritizing our connection with God and modeling his virtues in our lives, we have the power to leave behind a legacy that transcends generations.

In the stories of those who have gone before us, we find inspiration and guidance for our own journey. From the pages of scripture to the lives of saints and sages, we see examples of faithfulness, perseverance, and love that continue to inspire us today.

But our journey does not end here. As we close this book, let us carry forward the lessons we have learned and the vision we have cultivated. Let us commit ourselves anew to building a legacy that honors God and blesses our families and communities.

May we be courageous in our convictions, steadfast in our faith, and unwavering in our pursuit of righteousness. And may the legacy we leave behind be a testament to the grace and goodness of our Heavenly Father, who empowers us to live lives of purpose and significance.

As we step into the future with hope and confidence, let us remember that our legacy is not just about what we leave behind, but about the lives we touch and the hearts we transform along the way. May we walk in the footsteps of our Savior, Jesus Christ, and may his love guide us every step of the way.

With grateful hearts and eager anticipation, let us embrace the adventure of building a Godly legacy that will endure for eternity.

Lord, inspire and lead our actions and build a purpose-driven legacy. Amen.

ACKNOWLEDGMENT AND THANK YOU

With heartfelt gratitude, I extend my sincerest thanks to everyone who played a pivotal role in the journey of bringing 'Purpose-Driven Legacy' to life. Your support and encouragement have been invaluable.

First and foremost, I want to give thanks to our great and mighty Father above. Thank you, Lord, for the inspiration and guidance. All glory and Honor to God.

To my wife Sandra and my kids. Thank you so much for your love, support, and encouragement through this process and for the countless hours spent listening to me read this over and over again to you. To my wife Sandra, my rock of stability and the love of my life, you love so well, and I am so grateful to have you as my partner on this journey of life. To my oldest Dana, the one who made me a father and a grandfather. I love you and am so proud to be your daddy. To my little songbird Leah Joy, your heart for the Lord inspires me every day. To my son Elijah, my name's sake, I am so proud of the man you have become and pray your legacy is exponentially greater than mine. I love you all more than words could ever describe.

To my parents and in laws. David Royer, Darlene Brigham, Jon and Marla Johanson thank you for all the support and wisdom throughout my life.

To my sister Darah Joy, the one I grew up with and to the one person that will be present for more of my life than any other, I am so grateful for you. You are way smarter than me, but just SOMETIMES NOT ALWAYS. I'm number 1, number, number1... ha-ha (It's a sibling thing)

To my friends and family that helped to shape the narrative of my life story, I say thank you. I want to specifically call out a few friends that have walked beside me for years through thick and thin and have always been there for me when I needed them. Kirk Groff, Rob Greene, Adam Noll, Trent Moeller, Manny Lindo, Ryan Norris, Juan Fernandez, my nephew Paul Eagans, Alejo Buitrago, Mark Ellison, Robert Triplett, Troy Tyler, and Bradley Blomgren.

To my mentors, my father David Royer, my uncle Sam Pawlak, to my late grandfather Louis Davidson, and to my pastor and friend David Oates for your invaluable guidance and wisdom thank you from the bottom of my heart.

I also want to thank these men who have mentored me at different phases in my life. David Blomgren, Ken Collins, Greg Dumas, David Speicher, Williard Oates, Mike Paquin, Micah Brewer, Mark Owens, Paul Cliff, Clem Ferris, Jim Heldreth, Joseph Jones, Elmer Taylor, Doug Yates, Paul Portman, and many more.

To my publishing team, for your dedication and hard work – thank you from the bottom of my heart.

To the community that inspired these pages and to you, the readers, who have embarked on this journey with me – your engagement and enthusiasm are the very essence of this book's purpose. Thank you for being a part of this legacy."

Thank you,
Dustin Royer

APPENDIX

How to Pray *for* and *with* Your Wife
1. Pray that she would develop a deep love for the Lord God, dedicating her heart, mind, soul, and strength to Him. (Matt. 22:36–40).
2. Pray that she discovers her beauty and identity through her relationship with Christ, reflecting His character in her life. (1 Pet. 3:1–4, Prov. 31:30).
3. Pray that she embraces a love for the Word of God and permits its transformative power to nurture her growth. (Eph. 5:26).
4. Pray that she will exhibit grace, communicate truth with love, and refrain from engaging in gossip. (Eph. 4:15, Eph. 4:29, 1 Tim. 3:11).
5. Pray that she would honor you as her husband and willingly support your leadership as she does so unto the Lord. (Eph. 5:22–24).
6. Pray that she would cultivate gratitude and discover her contentment in Christ rather than in her circumstances. (Phil. 4:10–13).
7. Pray that she would demonstrate hospitality and be diligent in serving others with the joy that reflects Christ's character. (Phil. 2:3–4).
8. Pray that she contributes goodness to her family throughout her life, avoiding any actions that may bring harm or negativity. (Prov. 31:12, 1 Cor. 7:34).
9. Pray that she seeks out and welcomes the guidance of godly older women to mentor her, aiding in her growth. Also, pray that she becomes a godly mentor to her children and younger women. (Titus 3:4).
10. Pray that she remains steadfast in her roles as a wife and mother,

not succumbing to the lies of the enemy that seek to diminish her value in those roles. (Titus 2:5).
11. Pray that she embodies love, patience, resilience against offense, and a willingness to forgive quickly. (James 1:19, Eph. 4:32).
12. Pray that her intimate needs are fulfilled exclusively by you, her husband, and that she can reciprocate in meeting yours. (1 Cor. 7:1–5).
13. Pray that she remains devoted to prayer and is able to intercede effectively on behalf of others. (Col. 4:2, Luke 2:37).
14. Pray that she leads her home and guides her children diligently, reflecting the character of Christ in her actions. (Prov. 31:27).
15. Pray that there be no reason for her character to be slandered or to lose confidence. (1 Tim. 5:14).

How to Pray *for* and *with* Your Husband
1. Pray that he develops a deep love for the Lord, dedicating his heart, mind, soul, and strength to Him. (Matt. 22:36–40).
2. Pray that he walks with integrity, honoring his promises, and fulfilling his commitments. (Ps. 15, Ps. 112:1–9).
3. Pray that he loves you unconditionally and remains faithful to you. (Eph. 5:25–33, 1 Cor. 7:1–5).
4. Pray that he displays kindness, resilience against offense, and a willingness to forgive quickly. (James 1:19, Eph. 4:32).
5. Pray that he remains focused and avoids passivity, embracing responsibility with determination. (Neh. 6:1–14).
6. Pray that he becomes a diligent worker, faithfully providing for your family and children. (Prov. 6:6–11, 1 Tim. 5:8).
7. Pray that he surrounds himself with wise friends and steers clear of those who may lead him astray with foolishness. (Prov. 13:20, 1 Cor. 15:33).

8. Pray that he exercises sound judgment as he seeks justice, embraces mercy, and walks humbly with God. (Mic. 6:8).
9. Pray that he relies on God's wisdom and strength instead of his own. (Prov. 3:5, James 1:5, Phil. 2:13).
10. Pray that his decisions are rooted in reverence for God rather than fear of people. (Prov. 3:5, James 1:5, Phil. 2:13).
11. Pray that he grows into a strong spiritual leader, characterized by courage, wisdom, and unwavering conviction. (Josh. 1:1–10, Josh. 24:15).
12. Pray that he is liberated from any bondage, negative habits, or addictions that hinder his progress. (John 8:31, John 8:36, Rom. 6:1–19).
13. Pray that he discovers his identity and fulfillment in God rather than in temporary pleasures or possessions. (Psalms 37:4, 1 John 2:15–17).
14. Pray that he regularly reads and allows the Word of God to direct his choices and actions. (Ps. 119:105, Matt. 7:24–27).
15. Pray that he remains faithful to God and leaves behind a powerful legacy for future generations to follow. (2 Tim. 4:6–8, John 17:4).

SCRIPTURE INDEX

INTRODUCTION:

- No discipline seems enjoyable at the time, but painful. Later on, however, it yields the fruit of peace and righteousness to those who have been trained by it. (Hebrews 12:11)
- Apply yourself to discipline and listen to words of knowledge. (Proverbs 23:12)
- I have been crucified with Christ; it is no longer I who live, but Christ lives in me; and the life which I now live in the flesh, I live by faith in the Son of God, who loved me and delivered himself up for me. (Galatians 2:20)

MY JOURNEY:

- What was from the beginning, what we have heard, what we have seen with our eyes, what we have observed and have touched with our hands, concerning the word of life—that life was revealed, and we have seen it and we testify and declare to you the eternal life that was with the Father and was revealed to us—what we have seen and heard we also declare to you, so that you may also have fellowship with us; and indeed our fellowship is with the Father and with his Son, Jesus Christ. We are writing these things so that our joy may be complete. (1 John 1:1–4)
- Blessed is a man who perseveres under trial; for once he has been approved, he will receive the crown of life, which the Lord has promised to those who love him. (James 1:12)

GODLY LEGACY:

- We are the clay; you are the potter; we are all the work of your hand. (Isaiah 64:8)
- Once we were not a people, but now you are God's people; you had not received mercy, but now you have received mercy. (1 Peter 2:10)
- And you were dead in your trespasses and sins in which you previously lived according to the ways of this world, according to the ruler of the power of the air, the spirit now working in the disobedient. (Ephesians 2:1–2)
- We too all previously lived among them in the fleshly desires, carrying out the inclinations of our flesh and thoughts, and we were by nature children under wrath as the others were also. (Ephesians 2:3)
- Christ is head of the body, the church; he is the beginning, the firstborn from the dead, so that he might come to have first place in everything. For God was pleased to have all of his fullness dwell in him. (Colossians 1:18-19)
- But God, who is rich in mercy, because of his great love that he had for us, made us alive in Christ even though we were dead in trespasses. You are saved by Grace. (Ephesians 2:4–5)
- Abba, Father! All things are possible for you. Take this cup away from me. Nevertheless, not what I will, but what you will. (Mark 14:36)

PRIORITIES:

- For this reason, God highly exalted him and gave him the name that is above every name, so that at the name of Jesus every knee will bow—in heaven and on earth and under the earth—and

every tongue will confess that Jesus Christ is Lord, to the glory of God the Father. (Philippians 2:9–11)
- In the beginning was the Word, and the Word was with God, and the Word was God. (John 1:1-3)
- And the word was made flesh, and took residence amongst us; we observed His glory, the glory of the One and Only Son from the Father. (John 1:14)
- For although the law was given through Moses, grace and truth came through Jesus Christ. No one has ever seen God. The One and Only Son—the One who is at the Father's side—He has revealed Him. (John 1:17–18)
- I have spoken these things to you while I remain with you. But the Counselor, the Holy Spirit, whom the Father will send in my name, will teach you all things and remind you of everything I have told you. (John 14:25–26)
- Truly I tell you, the one who believes in me will also do the works that I do. And he will do even greater works than these, because I am going to the Father. Whatever you ask in my name, I will do it so that the Father may be glorified in the Son. If you ask me anything in my name, I will do it. (John 14:12–14)

PRIORITY 1: YOUR WALK WITH JESUS

- Therefore, you should pray like this: Our Father in heaven, your name be honored as holy. Your kingdom come. Your will be done on earth as it is in heaven. Give us today our daily bread. And forgive us our debts, as we also have forgiven our debtors. And do not bring us into temptation but deliver us from the evil one. (Matthew 6:9–13)

IDENTITY:

- Paul, a servant of Christ Jesus, called an apostle and set apart for the gospel of God. (Romans 1:1)
- Paul, called as an apostle of Christ Jesus by God's will. (1 Corinthians 1:1)
- Paul, an apostle of Christ Jesus by God's will. (2 Corinthians 1:1)
- Paul is an apostle—not from men or by man, but by Jesus Christ and God the Father, who raised him from the dead. (Galatians 1:1)
- Paul, an apostle of Christ Jesus by God's will: to the faithful saints in Christ Jesus. (Ephesians 1:1)
- Paul and Timothy, servants of Christ Jesus. (Philippians 1:1)
- Paul, an apostle of Christ Jesus by God's will. (Colossians 1:1)
- But you are a chosen generation, a royal priesthood, a holy nation, His own special people, that you may proclaim the praises of Him who called you out of the darkness into His marvelous light. (1 Peter 2:9)
- But of Him you are in Christ Jesus, who became for us wisdom from God—and righteousness and sanctification and redemption. (1 Corinthians 1:30)
- But sanctify the Lord God in your hearts, and always be ready to give a defense to everyone who asks you a reason for the hope that is in you, with meekness and fear. (1 Peter 3:15)
- For the Lord will not forsake His people, for His great name's sake, because it has pleased the Lord to make you His people. (1 Samuel 12:22)
- Therefore, as the elect of God, holy and beloved, put on tender mercies, kindness, humility, meekness, longsuffering. (Colossians 3:12)
- Having predestined us to adoption as sons by Jesus Christ to Himself, according to the good pleasure of His will. (Ephesians 1:5)

- For we are His workmanship, created in Christ Jesus for good works, which God prepared beforehand that we should walk in them. (Ephesians 2:10)
- There is neither Jew nor Greek, slave nor free, male nor female; for you are all one in Christ Jesus. (Galatians 3:28)
- Behold what manner of love the Father has bestowed on us, that we should be called children of God! Therefore, the world does not know us because it did not know him. (1 John 3:1)
- Now you are the body of Christ, and members individually. (1 Corinthians 12:27)
- The spirit of the Lord God is on me because the Lord has anointed me to bring good news to the poor. He has sent me to heal the brokenhearted, to proclaim liberty to the captives and freedom to the prisoners, to proclaim the year of the Lord's favor and the day of our God's vengeance; to comfort all who mourn, to provide for those who mourn in Zion; to give them a crown of beauty instead of ashes, festive oil instead of mourning and splendid clothes instead of despair. And they will be called righteous trees, planted by the Lord to glorify Him. (Isaiah 61:1–4)
- For all have sinned and fall short of the glory of God. (Romans 3:23)
- For the wages of sin is death, but the free gift of God is eternal life in Jesus Christ our Lord. (Romans 6:23)
- But God demonstrated His love towards us in that while we were yet sinners, Christ Jesus died for us. (Romans 5:8)
- For God so loved the world that, He gave his only begotten Son, that whosoever believes in Him should not perish, but have everlasting life. (John 3:16)
- For by Grace you have been saved through faith, and that not of ourselves, it is the gift of God. (Ephesians 2:8)
- That if you confess with your mouth Jesus as Lord, and believe in your heart that God raised Him from the dead, you will be

saved; for with the heart a person believes, resulting in righteousness, and with the mouth he confesses, resulting in salvation. (Romans 10:9–10)
- For by Grace you have been saved through faith. And this is not your own doing; it is the gift of God, not a result of works, so that no one may boast. For we are his workmanship, created in Christ Jesus for Good works, which God prepared beforehand, that we should walk in them. (Ephesians 2:8–10)

HEALING AND RESTORATION:

- Summoning his twelve disciples, he gave them authority over unclean spirits, to drive them out and to heal every disease and sickness. (Matthew 10:1)
- And the God of all grace, who called you to his eternal glory in Christ, after you have suffered a little while, will himself restore you and make you strong, firm and steadfast. (1 Peter 5:10)
- For all have sinned and fall short of the glory of God. They are justified through the redemption that is in Jesus Christ. (Romans 3:23–24)
- For this reason, God highly exalted him and gave him the name that is above every name, so that at the name of Jesus every knee will bow—In heaven and on earth—and every tongue will confess that Jesus Christ is Lord, to the glory of God the Father. (Philippians 2:9–11)
- Truly I tell you, the one who believes in me will also do the works that I do. And he will do even greater works than these, because I am going to the Father. Whatever you ask in my name, I will do it so that the Father may be glorified in the Son. If you ask me anything in my name, I will do it. (John 14:12–14)

- As far as the east is from the west, so far has he removed our transgressions from us. (Psalm 103:12)
- The eye is the lamp of the body. If your eye is healthy, your whole body will be full of light. But if your eye is bad, your whole body will be full of darkness. (Matthew 6:22–23)
- Indeed, the Protector of Israel does not slumber or sleep. The Lord protects you: the Lord is a shelter right by your side. (Psalm 121 4-5)
- After this, a Jewish festival took place, and Jesus went up to Jerusalem. By the Sheep Gate in Jerusalem there is a pool, called Bethesda in Aramaic, which has five colonnades. Within these lay a large number of the disabled—blind, lame, and paralyzed. One man was there who had been disabled for thirty-eight years. When Jesus saw him lying there and realized he had already been there a long time, he said to him, 'Do you want to get well?' 'Sir,' the disabled man answered, 'I have no one to put me into the pool when the water is stirred up, but while I'm coming, someone goes down ahead of me.' 'Get up,' Jesus told him, 'pick up your mat and walk.' Instantly, the man got well, picked up his mat, and started to walk. Now that day was the Sabbath, and so the Jews said to the man who had been healed, 'This is the Sabbath. The law prohibits you from picking up your mat.' He replied, 'The man who made me well told me, "Pick up your mat and walk."' 'Who is this man who told you, "Pick up your mat and walk"?' they asked. But the man who was healed did not know who it was because Jesus had slipped away into the crowd that was there. After this, Jesus found him in the temple and said to him, 'See, you are well. Do not sin anymore, so that something worse doesn't happen to you.' The man went and reported to the Jews that it was Jesus who had made him well. Therefore, the

Jews began persecuting Jesus because he was doing these things on the Sabbath. (John 5:1–16)

- While he was going, the crowds were nearly crushing him. A woman suffering from bleeding for twelve years, who had spent all she had on doctors and yet could not be healed by any, approached from behind and touched the end of his robe. Instantly her bleeding stopped. 'Who touched me?' Jesus asked. When they all denied it, Peter said, 'Master, the crowds are hemming you in and pressing against you.' 'Someone did touch me,' said Jesus. 'I know that power has gone out from me.' When the woman saw that she was discovered, she came trembling and fell down before him. In the presence of all the people, she declared the reason she had touched him and how she was instantly healed. 'Daughter,' he said to her, 'your faith has saved you. Go in peace. (Luke 8:42–48)

- When he entered Capernaum, a centurion came to him, pleading with him, 'Lord, my servant is lying at home paralyzed, in terrible agony.' He said to him, 'Am I to come and heal him?' 'Lord,' the centurion replied, 'I am not worthy to have you come under my roof. But just say the word, and my servant will be healed. For I too am a man under authority, having soldiers under my command. I say to this one, "Go," and he goes; and to another, "Come," and he comes; and to my servant, "Do this!" and he does it.' Hearing this, Jesus was amazed and said to those following him, 'Truly I tell you, I have not found anyone in Israel with so great a faith. I tell you that many will come from east and west to share the banquet with Abraham, Isaac, and Jacob in the kingdom of heaven. But the sons of the kingdom will be thrown into the outer darkness where there will be weeping and gnashing of teeth.' Then Jesus told the centurion, 'Go. As you

have believed, let it be done for you.' And his servant was healed that very moment. (Matthew 8:5–13)
- How can these things be?' asked Nicodemus. 'Are you a teacher of Israel and don't know these things?' Jesus replied. 'Truly I tell you, we speak what we know and we testify to what we have seen, but you do not accept our testimony. If I have told you about earthly things and you don't believe, how will you believe if I tell you about heavenly things?' (John 3:9–12)

PRIORITY 2: YOUR SPOUSE

- The heart of man reflects man. (Proverbs 27:19)
- As a person thinks in his heart, so is he. (Proverbs 23:7)
- Then the Lord God said, "It is not good for the man to be alone. I will make a helper corresponding to him." The Lord God formed out of the ground every wild animal and every bird of the sky and brought each to the man to see what he would call it. And whatever the man called a living creature, that was its name. The man gave names to all the livestock, to the birds of the sky, and to every wild animal; but for the man no helper was found corresponding to him. So the Lord God caused a deep sleep to come over the man, and he slept. God took one of his ribs and closed the flesh at that place. Then the Lord God made the rib he had taken from the man into a woman and brought her to the man. And the man said: This one, at last, is bone of my bone and flesh of my flesh; this one will be called "woman," for she was taken from man. This is why a man leaves his father and mother and bonds with his wife, and they become one flesh. Both the man and his wife were naked yet felt no shame. (Gen. 2:18–25)

- Haven't you read that he who created them, in the beginning, made them male and female, and he also said 'For this reason, a man will leave his father and mother and be joined to his wife, and the two will become one flesh. Therefore, what God has joined together, let no one separate. (Matthew 19:4-6)
- Teacher, which command in the law is the greatest?" He said to him, "Love the Lord your God with all your heart, with all your soul, and with all your mind. This is the greatest and most important command. The second is like it: Love your neighbor as yourself. All the Law and the Prophets depend on these two commands. (Matthew 22:36–40)
- In the same way, wives, submit yourselves to your own husbands so that, even if some disobey the word, they may be won over without a word by the way their wives live when they observe your pure, reverent lives. Don't let your beauty consist of outward things like elaborate hairstyles and wearing gold jewelry or fine clothes, but rather what is inside the heart—the imperishable quality of a gentle and quiet spirit, which is of great worth in God's sight. (1 Peter 3:1–4)
- Charm is deceptive and beauty is fleeting, but a woman who fears the Lord will be praised. (Proverbs 31:30)
- To make her holy, cleansing her with the washing of water by the word. (Ephesians 5:26)
- But speaking the truth in love, let us grow in every way into him who is the head—Christ. (Ephesians 4:15)
- No foul language should come from your mouth, but only what is good for building up someone in need, so that it gives grace to those who hear. (Ephesians 4:29)
- Wives, likewise, should be worthy of respect, not slanderers, self-controlled, faithful in everything. (1 Timothy 3:11)

- Wives, submit to your husbands as to the Lord, because the husband is the head of the wife as Christ is the head of the church. He is the Savior of the body. Now, as the church submits to Christ, so also wives are to submit to their husbands in everything. (Ephesians 5:22–24)
- I rejoiced in the Lord greatly because, once again, you renewed your care for me. You were, in fact, concerned about me but lacked the opportunity to show it. I don't say this out of need, for I have learned to be content in whatever circumstances I find myself. I know how to make do with little, and I know how to make do with a lot. In any and all circumstances, I have learned the secret of being content—whether well-fed or hungry, whether in abundance or in need. (Philippians 4:10–13)
- Do nothing out of selfish ambition or conceit, but in humility consider others as more important than yourselves. Everyone should look not to his own interests, but rather to the interests of others. (Philippians 2:3–4)
- She rewards him with good, not evil, all the days of her life. (Proverbs 31:12)
- And his interests are divided. The unmarried woman or virgin is concerned about the things of the Lord so that she may be holy both in body and in spirit. But the married woman is concerned about the things of the world—how she may please her husband. (1 Corinthians 7:34)
- In the same way, older women are to be reverent in behavior, not slanderers, not slaves to excessive drinking. They are to teach what is good, so that they may encourage the young women to love their husbands and to love their children. (Titus 3:4)
- To be self-controlled, pure, workers at home, kind, and in submission to their husbands, so that God's word will not be slandered. (Titus 2:5)

- My dear brothers and sisters, understand this: Everyone should be quick to listen, slow to speak, and slow to anger. (James 1:19)
- And be kind and compassionate to one another, forgiving one another, just as God also forgave you in Christ. (Ephesians 4:32)
- Now in response to the matters you wrote about: "It is good for a man not to have sexual relations with a woman." But because sexual immorality is so common, each man should have sexual relations with his own wife, and each woman should have sexual relations with her own husband. A husband should fulfill his marital duty to his wife, and likewise a wife to her husband. A wife does not have the right over her own body, but her husband does. In the same way, a husband does not have the right over his own body, but his wife does. Do not deprive one another—except when you agree for a time, to devote yourselves to prayer. Then come together again; otherwise, Satan may tempt you because of your lack of self-control. (1 Corinthians 7:1–5)
- Devote yourselves to prayer; stay alert in it with thanksgiving. (Colossians 4:2)
- And was a widow for eighty-four years. She did not leave the temple, serving God night and day with fasting and prayers. (Luke 2:37)
- She watches over the activities of her household and is never idle. (Proverbs 31:27)
- Therefore, I want younger women to marry, have children, manage their households, and give the adversary no opportunity to accuse us. (1 Timothy 5:14)
- "Teacher, which command in the law is the greatest?" He said to him, "Love the Lord your God with all your heart, with all your soul, and with all your mind. This is the greatest and most important command. The second is like it: Love your neighbor

as yourself. All the Law and the Prophets depend on these two commands." (Matthew 22:36–40)

- A Description of the Godly, A psalm of David. Lord, who can dwell in your tent? Who can live on your holy mountain? The one who lives blamelessly, practices righteousness, and acknowledges the truth in his heart—who does not slander with his tongue, who does not harm his friend or discredit his neighbor, who despises the one rejected by the Lord but honors those who fear the Lord, who keeps his word whatever the cost, who does not lend his silver at interest or take a bribe against the innocent—the one who does these things will never be shaken. (Psalm 15)
- The Traits of the Righteous Hallelujah! Happy is the person who fears the Lord, taking great delight in his commands. His descendants will be powerful in the land; the generation of the upright will be blessed. Wealth and riches are in his house, and his righteousness endures forever. Light shines in the darkness for the upright. He is gracious, compassionate, and righteous. Good will come to the one who lends generously and conducts his business fairly. He will never be shaken. The righteous one will be remembered forever. He will not fear bad news; his heart is confident, trusting in the Lord. His heart is assured; he will not fear. In the end he will look in triumph on his foes. He distributes freely to the poor; his righteousness endures forever. His horn will be exalted in honor. (Psalms 112:1–9)
- Husbands, love your wives, just as Christ loved the church and gave himself for her to make her holy, cleansing her with the washing of water by the word. He did this to present the church to himself in splendor, without spot or wrinkle or anything like that, but holy and blameless. In the same way, husbands are to love their wives as their own bodies. He who loves his wife loves

himself. For no one ever hates his own flesh but provides and cares for it, just as Christ does for the church, since we are members of his body. For this reason, a man will leave his father and mother and be joined to his wife, and the two will become one flesh. This mystery is profound, but I am talking about Christ and the church. To sum up, each one of you is to love his wife as himself, and the wife is to respect her husband. (Ephesians 5:25–33)

- Now in response to the matters you wrote about: "It is good for a man not to have sexual relations with a woman." But because sexual immorality is so common, each man should have sexual relations with his own wife, and each woman should have sexual relations with her own husband. A husband should fulfill his marital duty to his wife, and likewise a wife to her husband. A wife does not have the right over her own body, but her husband does. In the same way, a husband does not have the right over his own body, but his wife does. Do not deprive one another—except when you agree for a time, to devote yourselves to prayer. Then come together again; otherwise, Satan may tempt you because of your lack of self-control. (1 Corinthians 7:1–5)
- My dear brothers and sisters, understand this: Everyone should be quick to listen, slow to speak, and slow to anger. (James 1:19)
- And be kind and compassionate to one another, forgiving one another, just as God also forgave you in Christ. (Ephesians 4:32)
- Attempts to Discourage the Builders: When Sanballat, Tobiah, Geshem the Arab, and the rest of our enemies heard that I had rebuilt the wall and that no gap was left in it—though at that time I had not installed the doors in the city gates—Sanballat and Geshem sent me a message: "Come, let's meet together in the villages of the Ono Valley." They were planning to harm me. So I sent messengers to them, saying, "I am doing important work and cannot come down. Why should the work cease

while I leave it and go down to you?" Four times they sent me the same proposal, and I gave them the same reply. Sanballat sent me this same message a fifth time by his aide, who had an open letter in his hand. In it was written: It is reported among the nations—and Geshem agrees—that you and the Jews plan to rebel. This is the reason you are building the wall. According to these reports, you are to become their king and have even set up the prophets in Jerusalem to proclaim on your behalf, "There is a king in Judah." These rumors will be heard by the king. So come, let's confer together. Then I replied to him, "There is nothing to these rumors you are spreading; you are inventing them in your own mind." For they were all trying to intimidate us, saying, "They will drop their hands from the work, and it will never be finished." But now, my God, strengthen my hands. (Nehemiah 6:1–9)

- Attempts to Intimidate Nehemiah: I went to the house of Shemaiah son of Delaiah, son of Mehetabel, who was restricted to his house. He said: Let's meet at the house of God, inside the temple. Let's shut the temple doors because they're coming to kill you. They're coming to kill you tonight! But I said, "Should a man like me run away? How can someone like me enter the temple and live? I will not go." I realized that God had not sent him, because of the prophecy he spoke against me. Tobiah and Sanballat had hired him. He was hired, so that I would be intimidated, do as he suggested, sin, and get a bad reputation, in order that they could discredit me. My God, remember Tobiah and Sanballat for what they have done, and also the prophetess Noadiah and the other prophets who wanted to intimidate me. (Nehemiah 6:1–14)

- Go to the ant, you slacker! Observe its ways and become wise. Without leader, administrator, or ruler, it prepares its provisions in summer; it gathers its food during harvest. How long will you stay in bed, you slacker? When will you get up from your sleep? A little sleep, a little slumber, a little folding of the arms to rest, and your poverty will come like a robber, your need, like a bandit. (Proverbs 6:6–11)

- But if anyone does not provide for his own family, especially for his own household, he has denied the faith and is worse than an unbeliever. (1 Timothy 5:8)
- The one who walks with the wise will become wise, but a companion of fools will suffer harm. (Proverbs 13:20)
- Do not be deceived: "Bad company corrupts good morals." (1 Corinthians 15:33)
- Mankind, he has told each of you what is good and what it is the Lord requires of you: to act justly, to love faithfulness, and to walk humbly with your God. (Micah 6:8)
- Trust in the Lord with all your heart, and do not rely on your own understanding; in all your ways know him, and he will make your paths straight. (Proverbs 3:5)
- Now if any of you lacks wisdom, he should ask God—who gives to all generously and ungrudgingly—and it will be given to him. (James 1:5)
- God is working in you both to will and to work according to his good purpose. (Philippians 2:13)
- Trust in the Lord with all your heart, and do not rely on your own understanding; in all your ways know him, and he will make your paths straight. (Proverbs 3:5)
- Now if any of you lacks wisdom, he should ask God—who gives to all generously and ungrudgingly—and it will be given to him. (James 1:5)
- For it is God who is working in you both to will and to work according to his good purpose. (Philippians 2:13)

- After the death of Moses the Lord's servant, the Lord spoke to Joshua son of Nun, Moses's assistant: "Moses my servant is dead. Now you and all the people prepare to cross over the Jordan to the land I am giving the Israelites. I have given you every place where the sole of your foot treads, just as I promised Moses. Your territory will be from the wilderness and Lebanon to the great river, the Euphrates River—all the land of the Hittites—and west to the Mediterranean Sea. No one will be able to stand against you as long as you live. I will be with you, just as I was with Moses. I will not leave you or abandon you. "Be strong and courageous, for you will distribute the land I swore to their ancestors to give them as an inheritance. Above all, be strong and very courageous to observe carefully the whole instruction my servant Moses commanded you. Do not turn from it to the right or the left, so that you will have success wherever you go. This book of instruction must not depart from your mouth; you are to meditate on it day and night so that you may carefully observe everything written in it. For then you will prosper and succeed in whatever you do. Haven't I commanded you: be strong and courageous? Do not be afraid or discouraged, for the Lord your God is with you wherever you go." Then Joshua commanded the officers of the people." (Joshua 1:1–10)
- But if it doesn't please you to worship the Lord, choose for yourselves today: Which will you worship—the gods your ancestors worshiped beyond the Euphrates River or the gods of the Amorites in whose land you are living? As for me and my family, we will worship the Lord." (Joshua 24:15)
- Then Jesus said to the Jews who had believed him, "If you continue in my word, you really are my disciples." (John 8:31)
- So if the Son sets you free, you really will be free. (John 8:36)

- What should we say then? Should we continue in sin so that grace may multiply? Absolutely not! How can we who died to sin still live in it? Or are you unaware that all of us who were baptized into Christ Jesus were baptized into his death? Therefore, we were buried with him by baptism into death, in order that, just as Christ was raised from the dead by the glory of the Father, so we too may walk in newness of life. For if we have been united with him in the likeness of his death, we will certainly also be in the likeness of his resurrection. For we know that our old self was crucified with him so that the body ruled by sin might be rendered powerless so that we may no longer be enslaved to sin, since a person who has died is freed from sin. Now if we died with Christ, we believe that we will also live with him, because we know that Christ, having been raised from the dead, will not die again. Death no longer rules over him. For the death he died, he died to sin once for all time; but the life he lives, he lives to God. So, you too consider yourselves dead to sin and alive to God in Christ Jesus. Therefore do not let sin reign in your mortal body, so that you obey its desires. And do not offer any parts of it to sin as weapons for unrighteousness. But as those who are alive from the dead, offer yourselves to God, and all the parts of yourselves to God as weapons for righteousness. For sin will not rule over you, because you are not under the law but under grace. What then? Should we sin because we are not under the law but under grace? Absolutely not! Don't you know that if you offer yourselves to someone as obedient slaves, you are slaves of that one you obey—either of sin leading to death or of obedience leading to righteousness? But thank God that, although you used to be slaves of sin, you obeyed from the heart that pattern of teaching to which you were handed over, and having been set free from sin, you became enslaved to righteousness. I am using a human analogy because of the weakness of your flesh. For just as you offered the parts of yourselves as slaves to impurity, and to greater and greater lawlessness, so now offer them as slaves to righteousness, which results in sanctification. (Romans 6:1–19)

- Take delight in the Lord, and he will give you your heart's desires. (Psalms 37:4)
- Do not love the world or the things in the world. If anyone loves the world, the love of the Father is not in him. For everything in the world—the lust of the flesh, the lust of the eyes, and the pride in one's possessions—is not from the Father, but is from the world. And the world with its lust is passing away, but the one who does the will of God remains forever. (1 John 2:15–17)
- Your word is a lamp for my feet and a light on my path. (Psalms 119:105)
- "Therefore, everyone who hears these words of mine and acts on them will be like a wise man who built his house on the rock. The rain fell, the rivers rose, and the winds blew and pounded that house. Yet it didn't collapse, because its foundation was on the rock. But everyone who hears these words of mine and doesn't act on them will be like a foolish man who built his house on the sand. The rain fell, the rivers rose, the winds blew and pounded that house, and it collapsed. It collapsed with a great crash." (Matthew 7:24–27)
- For I am already being poured out as a drink offering, and the time for my departure is close. I have fought the good fight, I have finished the race, I have kept the faith. There is reserved for me the crown of righteousness, which the Lord, the righteous Judge, will give me on that day, and not only to me, but to all those who have loved his appearing. (2 Timothy 4:6–8)
- I have glorified you on the earth by completing the work you gave me to do. (John 17:4)

PRIORITY 3: YOUR FAMILY

- By the time he learns to reject what is bad and choose what is good, he will be eating butter and honey. (Isaiah 7:15)
- For before the boy knows to reject what is bad and choose what is good, the land of the two kings you dread will be abandoned. (Isaiah 7:16)
- The person who sins is the one who will die. A son won't suffer punishment for the father's iniquity, and a father won't suffer punishment for the son's iniquity. (Ezekiel 18:20)
- If my people, which are called by my name, shall humble themselves, and pray, and seek my face, and turn from their wicked ways; then will I hear from heaven, and will forgive their sin, and will heal their land. (2 Chronicles 7:14)

PRIORITY 4: YOUR WORK

- For the love of money is a root of all kinds of evil, and by craving it, some have wandered away from the faith and pierced themselves with many pains. (1 Tim. 6:10)
- Set your minds on what is above, not on what is on the earth" (Col. 3:2)
- Then God said, "Let us make man in our image, according to our likeness. They will rule the fish of the sea, the birds of the sky, the livestock, the whole earth, and the creatures that crawl on the earth. (Genesis 1:26)
- The Lord God took the man and placed him in the garden of Eden to work it and watch over it. (Genesis 2:15)
- Go to the ant, you slacker! Observe its ways and become wise. Without leader, administrator, or ruler, it prepares its provisions in summer; it gathers its food during harvest. How long will

you stay in bed, you slacker? When will you get up from your sleep? A little sleep, a little slumber, a little folding of the arms to rest, and your poverty will come like a robber, your need, like a bandit. (Proverbs 6:6–11)

- Complete your outdoor work and prepare your field; afterward, build your house. (Prov. 24:27)
- But if anyone does not provide for his own, that is his own household, he has denied the faith and is worse than an unbeliever. (1 Tim. 5:8)
- Now we command you, brothers, in the name of our Lord Jesus Christ, to keep away from every brother who walks irresponsibly and not according to the tradition received from us. For you yourselves know how you must imitate us: We were not irresponsible among you; we did not eat anyone's food free of charge; instead, we labored and struggled, working night and day, so that we would not be a burden to any of you. It is not that we don't have the right to support, but we did it to make ourselves an example to you so that you would imitate us. In fact, when we were with you, this is what we commanded you: "If anyone isn't willing to work, he should not eat." For we hear that there are some among you who walk irresponsibly, not working at all, but interfering with the work of others. Now we command and exhort such people by the Lord Jesus Christ that quietly working, they may eat their own food. Brothers, do not grow weary in doing good. (2 Thess. 3:6–12)
- On the seventh day God had completed his work that he had done, and he rested on the seventh day from all his work that he had done. (Gen. 2:2)
- Be still, and know that I am God, exalted among the nations, exalted on the earth (Ps. 46:10)

- For it is just like a man about to go on a journey. He called his own servants and entrusted his possessions to them. To one he gave five talents, to another two talents, and to another one talent, depending on each one's ability. Then he went on a journey. Immediately the man who had received five talents went, put them to work, and earned five more. In the same way the man with two earned two more. But the man who had received one talent went off, dug a hole in the ground, and hid his master's money. After a long time, the master of those servants came and settled accounts with them. The man who had received five talents approached, presented five more talents, and said, 'Master, you gave me five talents. See, I've earned five more talents.' "His master said to him, 'Well done, good and faithful servant! You were faithful over a few things; I will put you in charge of many things. Share your master's joy.' "The man with two talents also approached. He said, 'Master, you gave me two talents. See, I've earned two more talents.' His master said to him, 'Well done, good and faithful servant! You were faithful over a few things; I will put you in charge of many things. Share your master's joy.' "The man who had received one talent also approached and said, 'Master, I know you. You're a harsh man, reaping where you haven't sown and gathering where you haven't scattered seed. So I was afraid and went off and hid your talent in the ground. See, you have what is yours.' "His master replied to him, 'You evil, lazy servant! If you knew that I reap where I haven't sown and gather where I haven't scattered, then you should have deposited my money with the bankers, and I would have received my money back with interest when I returned. "'So, take the talent from him and give it to the one who has ten talents. For to everyone who has, more will be given, and he will have more than enough. But from the one who does not have, even what he has will be taken away from him. And throw this good-for-nothing servant into the outer darkness, where there will be weeping and gnashing of teeth.'" (Matt. 25:14–30)

PRIORITY 5: YOUR MINISTRY

- Above all, fear the LORD and worship him faithfully with all your heart; consider the great things he has done for you. (1 Samuel 12:24)
- Do not fear, for I am with you; do not be afraid, for I am your God. I will strengthen you, help you; I will hold on to you with my righteous right hand. (Isaiah 41:10)

PREPARATION FOR MINISTRY

- Preach the word; be ready in season and out of season; correct, rebuke, and encourage with great patience and teaching. (2 Timothy 4:2)

ELIJAH'S ENCOUNTER WITH GOD

- Suddenly, the word of the Lord came to him, and he said to him, "What are you doing here, Elijah?" He replied, "I have been very zealous for the Lord God of Armies, but the Israelites have abandoned your covenant, torn down your altars, and killed your prophets with the sword. I alone am left, and they are looking for me to take my life." Then he said, "Go out and stand on the mountain in the Lord's presence." At that moment, the Lord passed by. A great and mighty wind was tearing at the mountains and was shattering cliffs before the Lord, but the Lord was not in the wind. After the wind there was an earthquake, but the Lord was not in the earthquake. After the earthquake there was a fire, but the Lord was not in the fire. And after the fire there was a voice, a soft whisper. When Elijah heard it, he wrapped his face in his mantle and went out and stood at the entrance of the cave. Suddenly, a voice came to him and said, "What are you doing here, Elijah?" "I have been very zealous for the Lord God of Armies," he replied, "but the Israelites have abandoned your covenant, torn down your altars, and killed your prophets with the sword. I alone am left, and they're looking for me to take my life." Then the Lord said to him, "Go and return by the way you came to the Wilderness of Damascus. When you arrive, you are to anoint Hazael as king over Aram. You are to anoint Jehu son of Nimshi as king over Israel and Elisha son of Shaphat from Abel-meholah as prophet in your place. Then Jehu will put to death whoever escapes the sword of Hazael, and Elisha will put to death whoever escapes the sword of Jehu. But I will leave seven thousand in Israel—every knee that has not bowed to Baal and every mouth that has not kissed him." (1 Kings 19:9–18)

Dear Readers,

As the pages of "Purpose Driven Legacy" come to a close, the journey into living a life of intentional, God-centered purpose is just beginning. While writing this book, I felt a profound calling to extend the conversation and exploration into how we can continue to pursue God and build a godly legacy through our daily actions.

With gratitude and excitement, I am thrilled to announce the launch of a series of follow-up Bible studies designed to accompany "Purpose-Driven Legacy." These studies are crafted to deepen your understanding, spark meaningful reflection, and guide you in practical, scripture-based steps toward living a purposeful life that honors God.

What to Expect from the Bible Studies:

- **Deep Dives into Scriptural Themes:** Each study focuses on key themes from "Purpose-Driven Legacy," exploring them through the lens of scripture. Expect to uncover new insights and understandings of God's Word and how it applies to building a legacy.
- **Practical Applications:** Beyond theory, these studies are designed to be actionable. Each session includes questions and activities that encourage you to apply biblical principles to your daily life, ensuring your legacy is not just envisioned but actively built.
- **Community and Discussion:** Whether you're embarking on this journey solo or with a group, these studies are a gateway to meaningful discussions. Share insights, challenges, and victories with others who are committed to living purposefully for God.

How to Access the Bible Studies:
The Bible studies are available directly through my Amazon author page: [Dustin Royer on Amazon](https://amazon.com/author/dustinroyer). Here, you can view and purchase the study guides individually or as a complete set. Each guide is designed to stand alone, allowing you to engage with them in any order that speaks to your heart.

A Personal Invitation:
I invite you, dear reader, to continue your journey of discovery and growth through these Bible studies. It is my prayer that they serve as a valuable tool in your quest to live a life that not only seeks God's purpose but actively contributes to a legacy that honors Him.

Thank you for allowing "Purpose Driven Legacy" to be a part of your spiritual journey. May these follow-up studies further enrich your walk with God, guiding you to deeper understanding, renewed purpose, and a legacy that truly reflects His love and glory.

With warmth and blessings,
Dustin Royer

www.ingramcontent.com/pod-product-compliance
Lightning Source LLC
LaVergne TN
LVHW021828060526
838201LV00058B/3552